ALMOST GONE

TWENTY-FIVE DAYS AND ONE CHANCE
TO SAVE OUR DAUGHTER

John Baldwin and Mackenzie Baldwin

Introduction by Stephanie Baldwin

HOWARD BOOKS
AN IMPRINT OF SIMON & SCHUSTER, INC.

NEW YORK   LONDON   TORONTO   SYDNEY   NEW DELHI

Howard Books
An Imprint of Simon & Schuster, Inc.
1230 Avenue of the Americas
New York, NY 10020

Copyright © 2017 by Mackenzie Baldwin, John Baldwin, and Stephanie Baldwin

Certain names have been changed, including those of Aadam and his family and the individuals at the mosque.

All rights reserved, including the right to reproduce this book or portions thereof in any form whatsoever. For information, address Howard Books Subsidiary Rights Department, 1230 Avenue of the Americas, New York, NY 10020.

First Howard Books hardcover edition November 2017

HOWARD and colophon are trademarks of Simon & Schuster, Inc.

For information about special discounts for bulk purchases, please contact Simon & Schuster Special Sales at 1-866-506-1949 or business@simonandschuster.com.

The Simon & Schuster Speakers Bureau can bring authors to your live event. For more information or to book an event, contact the Simon & Schuster Speakers Bureau at 1-866-248-3049 or visit our website at www.simonspeakers.com.

Interior design by Kyoko Watanabe

Manufactured in the United States of America

10 9 8 7 6 5 4 3 2 1

Library of Congress Cataloging-in-Publication Data is available.

ISBN 978-1-5011-7904-4
ISBN 978-1-5011-7906-8 (ebook)

Dedicated to
Jordyn, Sarah, and Madison

CONTENTS

INTRODUCTION BY *Stephanie Baldwin*   ix

CHAPTER 1: Facing the FBI—*Mackenzie and John*   1

CHAPTER 2: Shifting Winds—*John*   11

CHAPTER 3: Safety Nets—*John*   21

CHAPTER 4: A Harmless Meeting—*Mackenzie*   29

CHAPTER 5: Growing Attachments—*Mackenzie*   35

CHAPTER 6: Making Plans—*Mackenzie*   41

CHAPTER 7: Examining Faith—*John and Mackenzie*   45

CHAPTER 8: Twisting Scripture—*John*   53

CHAPTER 9: Burden Shared—*John and Mackenzie*   61

CHAPTER 10: Deeper into His World—*John and Mackenzie*   71

CHAPTER 11: A Second Family—*Mackenzie*   79

CONTENTS

CHAPTER 12: Love Her Where She's At—*John*   87

CHAPTER 13: Change of Plans—*Mackenzie and John*   95

CHAPTER 14: Lightning Strikes—*John*   105

CHAPTER 15: Cat and Mouse—*John*   115

CHAPTER 16: Alarming Discoveries—*John and Mackenzie*   123

CHAPTER 17: A Father's Love—*John*   131

CHAPTER 18: A Plan to Save Her—*John*   139

CHAPTER 19: Confirmation—*Mackenzie*   147

CHAPTER 20: Moment of Truth—*John*   153

CHAPTER 21: Denial—*John*   165

CHAPTER 22: Fighting for Her Heart and Soul—*John*   173

CHAPTER 23: Coming Storm—*John*   183

CHAPTER 24: An Angel Leads the Way—*John and Mackenzie*   191

CHAPTER 25: Acceptance—*John and Mackenzie*   201

APPENDIX: Understanding and Helping Loved Ones Who Are in Unhealthy Relationships—*Cheryl La Mastra*   211

ACKNOWLEDGMENTS   225

INTRODUCTION

Stephanie Baldwin

It's not easy sharing our story—at least it wasn't at first. Our family is much more than this one crisis year, yet this one year nearly destroyed all that we had built and cherished.

Throughout half of that year, my husband, John, and I kept silent about what we were going through. We struggled and prayed alone. When we finally did tell our closest family and friends, we were humbled by their support, love, and prayers and realized just how much we needed them. We saw God bring just the right people, at just the right moments, into our lives. Then the bravery of three girls who spoke up proved to be an essential piece in saving our daughter, Mackenzie.

We came within mere days of losing our daughter forever. She was victimized by someone she thought she knew, but didn't. In the pursuit of this relationship, she cast aside her faith, her family, and her closest friends. *Almost Gone* is the story of how all this unfolded and how our precious daughter was ultimately saved.

When it was over, Mackenzie was safe, but she was distraught, embarrassed, and confused as to what she had done and why she had done it. It took time for her to heal and come to grips with what had happened. Forgiving herself was the hardest part. Mack found herself at a crossroads: she could spend her life trying to hide from what had happened, or she could take ownership of it. She chose to own it.

We wrote *Almost Gone* to share what happened to our family so that other young people will not repeat the mistakes Mackenzie made, and to give the parents of those young people hope that through God's love and grace, anything can happen. I am immensely proud of how Mackenzie regularly shares her side of this story with both small and large groups of people in an unvarnished and authentic way. Today, as I watch our brave and adventurous daughter telling her story around the country, I marvel at God's hand at work in the smallest details to save her from almost certain disaster.

We see *Almost Gone* as our way to help other families realize that things are not always as perfect as they look from the outside, that individuals can make a profound difference in other people's lives, and that love and forgiveness can transcend every barrier. The story is told from two perspectives—John's and Mackenzie's, father and daughter. We hope this will allow you to experience John's and my perspectives as parents whose daughter changed dramatically in ways we didn't understand; and understand our daughter's point of view as she reveals how and why she was nearly lured away.

Mackenzie's story will allow you to see inside our daughter's mind—the mind of a very strong-willed and independent young woman—as she was slowly manipulated and enticed away from her family, her faith, and even herself. From the moment any parent first holds their newborn, their greatest fear is losing that precious child, or of harm coming to him or her. We came very close to that fear becoming our reality.

One night, after everything was over and Mackenzie was safe, we had company who stayed over, so John and I ended up using Mack's old bedroom for the night. I found myself staring through the darkness at the photographs of her days at camps, horseback riding, and four-wheeling. Sprinkled among them were spiritual and inspirational messages, as well as photos of family vacations and happy memories. I felt tears welling up as I wondered how, though we had done so much together, she had been so willing to leave it all. *Where did we go wrong?* I asked myself. Later, I came to realize that those memories were the foundation of love and faith that allowed us to survive and heal as a family. We spent years building that foundation, and when it counted, the foundation held strong. I know that not every story has a happy ending. Even in the strongest families with solid foundations, a child can make choices that have tragic results. But if our story can help even one family have better insights into potential dangers and how to navigate them, we will have accomplished our goal.

Our perspective is one picture of the journey, challenges, heart-aches, and confusion parents experience when a child is in crisis. We also hope it shows that partnership in marriage, unconditional love, and the generosity of friends and strangers are gifts from God to help us weather the storms we face as parents.

Our entire family feels that God has given us a responsibility to speak up. We pray that by telling our story, God's hand of guidance will be revealed, and that other families will be encouraged, com-forted, and offered help in their own times of trouble.

Friends leaning on friends through the sharing of our most in-timate times builds trust and relationships. I was reminded of this truth while I was shopping in a local store, where I happened to see a retired couple from our church. We made small talk for a few minutes, and I asked them to pray for Mackenzie because she "just isn't where she should be spiritually." The great reward for me came when they shared their story of their own daughter's struggle years earlier. They explained that they were always trying to "fix things," but they eventually realized that God wanted them to "get out of His way" and allow Him to reach their daughter. Their story made me realize that perhaps I, in the midst of our crisis, needed to "get out of His way" and allow God to handle it. From that day on, I changed my prayer from "God, please change her" to "God, tell me what You want me to do."

Our remarkable journey has taught our family that despite the hardships we encounter, God is *always* faithful, even when we can't see Him for a time. For Mackenzie, she rediscovered God's faithfulness and love even after she had turned away. As parents, we learned to love our daughter no matter what, and to love her where she's at. Through it all, we discovered that God loves us no matter what, and He loves us where we're at.

CHAPTER 1

Facing the FBI

Mackenzie Baldwin

I had kept the dark secret for nearly a year. My plan was ready, and in three days I would be leaving behind everything I knew in my hometown of Plano, Texas—my loving mother and father, my two younger brothers, and the friends and relatives I'd grown up with— to travel across the world to an unknown land. Finally, all that I had worked tirelessly toward and sacrificed for was about to be worth it.

Or so I believed. I have no idea what might have happened to me if those three days had gone as planned. Where would I be today? Would I have seen my parents, brothers, and friends again? Would I even be alive? Was I really three days away from walking into something I wouldn't have been able to walk out of?

Instead of packing my suitcases and preparing to leave on that fateful day in June 2014, I sat at the dining room table in my house with three FBI agents and my parents. I'd sat at this table a thousand times in my eighteen years, eating meals with my family, laughing and joking with them, and praying together, but I never imagined something like this. I couldn't believe FBI agents were sitting at our dining room table, and they were there to talk to *me*. It was like a scene out of a Hollywood thriller—and somehow I was the suspect.

"Mackenzie, if you lie to us, we will know," said the FBI agent across the table. "We already know the answers to most of the questions we are about to ask."

My mind raced over what had transpired during the past several months, and I tried to remember everything I had done to determine what laws I might have broken and why these FBI agents were there to talk to me. Although I can usually handle almost anything thrown my way, I have to admit that I was scared. I had deceived my parents and closest friends, keeping many secrets from them and carefully covering my tracks every step of the way, but I didn't think I'd done anything that would have constituted a crime—or so I hoped.

Dad sat at the end of the table, and Mom had the chair to my left. Thankfully, my younger brothers and grandparents were nowhere in sight, but I wished my parents weren't there. I felt sure truths would soon be revealed, and I didn't want to hurt them with the revelations of what I'd done and what I planned to do. I didn't think my parents knew anything about my plans to leave or what was luring me away from them. More than anything, I didn't want to see their disappointment when they learned the extent of my lies and deception.

My parents' somber faces reflected the seriousness of this moment. Dad looked exhausted and, though he sat stoically, he had the appearance of someone who had been kicked in the gut. I had done that proverbial kicking, and my heart truly ached for him. How could our relationship have changed so much in only a year? We had always been so close. Growing up, I'd spent a lot of time with him camping, backpacking, white-water rafting, and rock-climbing, and during those wonderful times together, we talked about practically everything. He took advantage of every opportunity to spend time with me, and I truly appreciated his selflessness and loved him for it.

Dad has a presence about him that others might consider intimidating, but I'd always viewed it as protective and had never doubted that he put our family first. We had once been inseparable, but now there was a great and growing distance between us, so much so that I was intent on leaving the country without my parents' knowledge. As I sat there, I wished I could take back all the pain I had caused them over the past year, but I still didn't want to change my plans or for my parents to find out why I had drifted so far away from them and our family.

The men at the table had introduced themselves, but I couldn't remember their names. The one who first spoke seemed to be in charge. He was probably six feet three inches tall and looked like a stereotypical FBI agent: well groomed; fit; wearing a dark suit, white shirt, and conservative tie. He studied me with hard, probing eyes, as if he could read my thoughts. I'd never so much as met an FBI agent, let alone had three of

> The one who first spoke seemed to be in charge. He was probably six feet three inches tall and looked like a stereotypical FBI agent.

them staring me down. I trembled in my seat and shoved my hands under my thighs to keep them from shaking. I did not want the agents to notice that I was flustered.

On the floor at my feet, my messenger bag held a replacement passport with my name on it. A passport I had lied to get. My mind was spinning with how I could still go through with my plan to leave. I was so close to being gone. When I had walked out of my final exams earlier that day, I was shocked to see Mom waiting in the Plano West Senior High School parking lot by my car. *That's weird,* I'd thought, as I tried to conjure up a normal enough smile.

"The FBI is at the house, and they want to talk to you," Mom said.

"Why?" This made no sense at all. Yes, I had hidden secrets from my parents, but I couldn't think of anything I'd done that would bring the FBI to our door. Other students were streaming toward their cars around us.

"You are eighteen, so they won't talk to me. Do you have any idea why they'd be there?"

"No," I told her, which wasn't completely true. I just didn't know what I'd done that might be considered a crime.

The drive from my high school to home was mostly silent. Mom told me to drive, and she climbed into the passenger seat. My car was a white Mazda Tribute with a manual transmission, but I didn't want to drive. I needed to use my phone, but now I couldn't. When we turned down our street, I saw three dark sedans parked in front of the house. The walk to our front door was the longest walk ever. Inside, the three agents were at the table with Dad.

They pushed back their chairs as they stood, reached out, and politely shook my hand. They pulled out their credentials and introduced themselves as I tried to get my bearings.

I glanced at the door. There seemed little chance I could get out of this.

After we sat down, one of the agents explained how they'd know if I was lying. The one opposite my dad pulled out a paper and set it on the table as the agent in charge said, "This states your Miranda rights. This is what we would use to take you out of here in handcuffs. We don't want to do that, so it is important that you answer all of our questions honestly."

I glanced at the door. There seemed little chance I could get out of this. But I couldn't let go of my plan. I was so wrapped up in the secrets and lies that I couldn't see anything but one direction. Even as I began to answer questions from special agents of the FBI, I was as determined as ever to get out of there and get on an airplane.

John Baldwin

My little girl was sitting at our table with my wife, Stephanie, and three FBI agents, and the staggering weight of what had been a very difficult year fell hard over me. My thoughts turned to two things: first, *Thank you, God!* that we were at this table instead of the horrible alternatives; and then, *How did it come to this?*

The fact that we were here was surreal. Stephanie and I had dedicated our lives to our children, our church, and our community. In a matter of months, however, the daughter we knew so well suddenly behaved like a complete stranger. She'd pushed us away and shut us out of her life. She had abandoned the friends she'd known for much of her life, as well as the Christian faith she was introduced to when she was six weeks old. We were consumed in a fight for Mackenzie's heart and soul, and even her life.

As the FBI agents questioned Mackenzie, I could see the fear and panic in her dark eyes despite how she fought to remain strong and calm. Stephanie describes her as stubborn, adventurous, outgoing, and, well, stubborn. Those traits are what make her so appealing to others; she's fun to be around and always had a strong corps of friends. She was also independent and strong-willed, even when she was a very young child. Facing the FBI agents, however, Mackenzie suddenly appeared small. My thoughts went back to the day Stephanie and I had joyfully welcomed this baby girl into our lives after ten years of marriage.

How different things were eighteen years ago. Stephanie and I had a goal of building a family with strong bonds and a sound Christian foundation. At Mackenzie's birth, we dedicated ourselves to being a family that served God and was involved in our church and community. We wanted to do everything we could to be the best parents possible. Even then, I understood the fleeting nature of time, and I was determined that Mackenzie's youngest years were not going to be lost on me. As a new dad, I believed that now was the time to start making an impression on our precious, innocent daughter. Her heart and mind were a blank tape, and the more I impressed on them, the more good she'd absorb.

The first course of business was to make "Dada" her first word. Day after day, I'd prop her up face-to-face with me on the floor and repeat, "Dada . . . Dada . . . Dada . . . Dada . . . ," then I'd throw in a single "Ma" for balance. Soon every man, woman, and child that Mackenzie met was known as "Dada"—victory was mine!

Our home church, Wilshire Baptist Church in Dallas, had a powerful tradition where families dedicated their new babies to be raised under the principles of Christian love and grace. For this event, we carefully selected a Bible verse to serve as our daughter's life verse and as our pledge to our infant daughter. We chose 2 Corinthians 9:15, "Thanks be to God for his indescribable gift."

On the Sunday morning of her dedication, our pastor, Dr. George Mason, read Mackenzie's verse and, while carrying her in his arms, walked up and down the church aisle looking directly into her eyes. "Your mom and dad are going to raise you to be a strong Christian young woman, and right now I ask God to bless your life and use it for a special purpose, for the sake of serving our Lord Jesus Christ," he told her. George also charged Stephanie and me with the responsibility of doing everything in our power to ensure that Mackenzie grew up with this focus. That morning, I felt the weight of responsibility and gladly accepted it.

A few months later, we purchased an heirloom clock and inscribed the brass pendulum with MJB—Mackenzie Jill Baldwin. Her middle-name namesake, Jill, is my younger sister, who embodies the attributes of love, generosity, gentleness, and kindness that

Stephanie and I hoped to inspire in Mackenzie. Inside the door of the clock, on its base, a small brass plate was inscribed with her life verse—2 Corinthians 9:15. We hung the clock in our dining room as a constant reminder as Mackenzie grew up.

All these years later, here we sat at our family dining room table. Our daughter had turned away from her Christian faith, saying she didn't believe anymore. She had lied to us countless times, plotted behind our backs, and she *wanted* to leave us.

Today could go in any direction, and for a moment I just wished it would all go away. The whole year had been terribly nerve-wracking, turning from awful to critical when another father called me less than a month ago. He'd said, "There's no good way to say this, John. I'm really sorry . . ."

That friend and fellow father then unveiled a stunning truth that launched us into a critical twenty-five-day period to not only save Mackenzie's future, but potentially her life. Our daughter was plotting and planning, trusting one young man whom she barely knew. She had no idea of the real truth. Even though I felt betrayed and heartbroken, I was as determined as ever that we would save our daughter—whatever the cost—even if that meant saving her from herself.

> I was determined that we would save our daughter—whatever the cost—even if that meant saving her from herself.

As I looked at my little girl, I felt overwhelming gratitude that she was there and not gone, as I'd feared for the past month. Without that phone call and three of Mack's close friends coming forward, we wouldn't be here now—only three days before she planned to leave us. This was the moment of truth that Stephanie and I had worked tirelessly for in the past twenty-two days, or perhaps, more accurately, for the eighteen years since we'd chosen Mack's life verse.

Thank God Mack was here at this table and not in some faraway place. For a moment, it felt as if time stopped before the questions began. A clock ticked in the background—the heirloom clock with our daughter's life verse inscribed inside. In that moment, I reflected on that verse again, but for a wholly different reason. *Thanks be to God for his indescribable gift.* It was a blessing that my daughter was still here.

However, my little girl wasn't safe yet. It had taken a miracle to get to this moment, but more miracles were needed to keep her safe and bring her heart back home.

I felt exhausted and hurt and angry. But more than that, I felt love for my daughter. I'd never give up on her, no matter how this turned out.

CHAPTER 2

Shifting Winds

John

Nearly a year before Mackenzie's meeting with the FBI agents in our home, she asked me a question I never thought I'd hear come from her mouth.

"Dad, would it be all right if I buy a Koran?"

It was a typical warm June day in Plano, Texas, soon after the end of Mack's junior year of high school. I was working from home when Mackenzie came down the stairs to my office door. Stephanie and I had recently reflected that Mack's junior year had been her happiest and most successful. She had a good group of friends, was working at her beloved exotic bird store, and had earned pretty good grades. By working extra side jobs, she'd even saved her money and purchased a beautiful green-winged macaw named Indy. Seeing our daughter set and achieve goals on her own was an encouraging sign of her growing maturity. She was becoming a responsible, more caring, and trustworthy young woman.

After a few challenging years, she now had earned our complete trust. We looked ahead to her eighteenth birthday in the fall and a senior year that would surely be filled with her friends coming in and out of our house like they always did. We'd have our younger sons' activities too. Luke was in the eighth grade, and Michael, fifth. Luke had an upcoming role in the production of *Thoroughly Modern Millie*, and Michael was playing baseball. Both were in High Adventure Treks (HATS) with me, just as Mack had been from grades five through nine. High Adventure Treks is a nonprofit organization that helps fathers and their sons and daughters strengthen their relationship and communication by conquering high adventure challenges as a team in a variety of outdoor settings. I loved completing activities such as canoeing, rock-climbing, rappelling, white-water kayaking, backpacking, and camping with Mack, and I was so looking forward to interacting with my sons in the outdoors too. HATS activities offered a great palette for us to learn how to communicate with each other. We also had our usual church involvement. The coming school year would be busy and hectic and altogether what typical families like ours enjoyed.

What Stephanie and I were most grateful for was that Mack was happy. But now her request to buy a Koran, the central religious text of Islam, caught me by surprise. Before I was able to ask Mack why she wanted to buy a Koran, she said, "I just want to compare it with the Bible." My immediate thought was *Absolutely not!* We are Christians, and I wasn't sure comparing our faith to Islam was a good idea. However, experience had taught me to refrain from an immediate response and hear her out. Mack could be unyieldingly headstrong

> Mack's request to buy a Koran, the central religious text of Islam, caught me by surprise.

when she felt her position was being unjustly questioned, and when that happened, it usually led to a healthy argument. I also recognized that Mack didn't have to ask me about it at all. She could have easily purchased a Koran at Barnes & Noble and I would never have known otherwise. The fact that she was willing to ask my opinion and engage in a conversation about it was, in my view, a good thing. Besides, with Mack, the forbidden was often more appealing than the allowed.

Raising Mackenzie was a lot like Texas weather. In Texas, we have beautiful spring days with crystal-blue skies, puffy white clouds, and cool light breezes. But, in the space of only a few hours, you can feel a sudden shift in the wind. The skies darken with booming thunder and dangerous lightning, and everyone is forced to seek shelter from the incoming thunderstorm. On occasion, a spring storm can also spawn supercells with damaging winds, large-sized hail, and even deadly tornadoes. And when you find yourself in a tornado's destructive path, all you can do is find a safe place to hide and pray for it to pass.

My daughter has many facets to her vibrant personality. On the positive side, Mack is resourceful and hardworking. In middle school, she obtained a permit to paint address numbers on curbs for $10 each. Later she started a face-painting business and worked at birthday parties and daycare summer camps. Swimming was her passion because she so badly wanted to work with whales and dolphins. She swam for a local swim club several days a week, which led her to secure her lifeguarding certification, teach swimming lessons, and work as a lifeguard at the local recreation center. Being a young entrepreneur fit her personality; she was never afraid to take on challenges. She was a determined girl, and she viewed roadblocks as something meant to jump, climb, or knock over.

Now, make no mistake, I dearly love my daughter. But bless her heart, she was not an easy kid to raise. Starting in the seventh grade, Mack was intently bored with school, and she was not one to allow her schoolwork to intrude on her social life. Mack longed to be more worldly and experienced than her friends, but her naïveté resulted in quite a few hard landings. During her middle school years, Mack pushed back on just about everything—homework, church, choice of friends, and the way she talked to her younger brothers. The list went on and on. Interspersed in the constant teenage girl drama was my funny, likable, adventurous, and spontaneous daughter, who somehow made all the hard times more or less balance out. Stephanie has often told me that I was Mack's "halo straightener," and believe me, that halo was not always shiny and it was seldom straight!

Our most difficult times with Mack probably occurred when she was a freshman in high school. The school year started out promising, but then she became drawn to a group of kids who were fun but troubled. Fortunately, Mackenzie had a line she wouldn't cross. We never had to deal with her experimenting with drugs or alcohol, but the relationships were unhealthy and impacted her in other ways. Her grades fell, her attitude eroded, and things became pretty difficult for us at home. To address Mackenzie's poor choices, we enforced a few months of "tough love" in an effort to curtail this latest episode of teenage rebellion. We also decided to seek family counseling with her and, fortunately, we successfully moved past this rebellious stage just before the school year ended.

Only a few weeks later, Mack and I went on our long-anticipated HATS Colorado trek. While many of the fathers and daughters there experienced a transcendent ten days together, our experience was anything but that. Our relationship was badly bruised from the previous six months of acrimony, and it was impossible to keep the hard feelings from creeping in during our time together, no matter how hard I tried. Thankfully, we had some joyous times on the trip, including a thirty-foot jump from a telephone pole, followed by a memorable hug and thank-you from Mack.

That summer, Mack felt a little unsettled by her experiences the previous school year, and she asked Stephanie what she needed to do differently in the future. Stephanie emphasized the importance of placing character, spirituality, and integrity at the top of her list of attributes when building any relationship. Mack took her mother's advice to heart, and a new window of hope opened for us as we headed into her sophomore year.

Anxious to start anew, Mack engaged a new group of friends during her sophomore year and experienced some of her happiest times. The episodes of the dark and angry freshman dissolved and were replaced with a consistently carefree, free-spirited young woman hanging out with her friends and enjoying life. They played hide-and-seek on the local golf course, and went to the movies, roller-skating, and dances. They really seemed to enjoy each other's company, and Stephanie and I approved of her new friends. One day that summer, we piled them into our truck and took them boating and water-skiing. Most nights, they'd end up back at our house, playing Xbox or watching scary movies for hours. Mack and her best friend, Madison, also became more involved at church, which was a very encouraging sign for her mother and me. For the first time as a teenager, Mack was showing a genuine interest in her Christian beliefs.

> Anxious to start anew, Mack engaged a new group of friends during her sophomore year and experienced some of her happiest times.

By now we knew Mackenzie wanted to take a gap year before starting college, and we fully agreed with her. She wasn't interested in starting college right away and we knew it would be a waste of time and money for us to force her to go. Ever the adventurer, Mackenzie wanted to take a postgraduation trip to Europe and backpack through the countryside. Naturally, we were not comfortable with the idea, but we hoped a trip to Europe would motivate her to finish her senior year strong and provide her an incentive to work a few more hours to save money. As a compromise, we agreed that she would stay with friends who lived in Switzerland and do some short day trips from there. A couple of years prior, Mackenzie had become friends with a Swiss foreign exchange student named Miriam, who had lived with Stephanie's sister, Debbie, for about a year. They had stayed in contact with each other through Facebook posts and an occasional text message since then. Knowing the family, we were confident they would take great care of Mackenzie when she arrived in Zurich.

The plan was for Mackenzie to fly directly to Zurich, where our friends would pick her up and have her stay with them for a week or so. As long as Mackenzie stayed in Switzerland and kept in touch with our friends, she would be allowed to stay in youth hostels and do some independent sightseeing. She had to earn the money for the trip herself, but we intended to help her out if she came up a little short, as part of her graduation present. It seemed like a good, safe way for her to do something special and provide her a bit of the independence she so craved.

But then, on that warm June day in 2013, Mack stood outside my office door asking me if she could purchase a Koran. For all her interests and passions, she'd never been interested in religious studies. Several months earlier the subject of religion arose, and she made a comment about Islam and how it seemed to be such a peaceful religion. She said she wished Christianity could be more that way. It seemed like an odd comment coming from someone who was raised in a Christian home and had never shown much interest in other faiths.

"Why do you think it's a peaceful religion?" I asked her.

In the shadow of 9/11, the Iraq War, and the loss of so many innocent lives at the hands of Islamic terrorists, I was somewhat suspicious. But I of course recognized that not all Muslims could or should be painted by the same broad brush.

"Oh, I know a couple of girls at school who are Muslim," Mack replied. "They just seem so peaceful. It just seems nice. You don't see Muslim kids doing the same things Christian kids do."

As Mack stood with one foot on the stairs to go up to her room, I tried not to come across too harshly when I expressed to her my concerns. I didn't know a lot about Islam, but I did know Muslims had some very different beliefs. I also pointed out to her that Islam had a history of intolerance—including its treatment of women—that went back hundreds if not thousands of years.

"Don't be fooled into thinking that these two girls, as nice as I'm sure they and their families are, represent the whole of the Muslim world," I told her. "There are some within that religion who do not get along with anyone except other Muslims, and only those of the same sect."

I saw a small flash of annoyance on Mack's face. "Dad, you can't judge all Muslims the same way."

"I'm not, you just have to be careful."

We didn't discuss it long, and upstairs she ran.

I thought her interest in Islam was a little curious, but I didn't worry about it too much. She was defending her friends, and I knew that. West Plano was experiencing a demographic shift with a recent influx of Middle Eastern residents, driven by the high-paying technical jobs supported in the Dallas/Fort Worth metropolitan area. Stephanie and I had always encouraged our kids to be kind toward and accepting of other people without bias toward different cultures or religions. But we stressed the importance of being grounded in our own faith.

I also knew my daughter's Christian journey had been hot and cold. While our Christian faith is prominent in our family, it didn't permeate every discussion and decision with our kids. We tried to raise our family by example. We showed the importance of our Christian faith through our involvement in Bible studies and by volunteering our time in church ministries. We prayed as a family, attended church regularly, and set examples for our children by relying on Christ during times of crisis. After being so involved with her youth group the summer of her sophomore year, Mackenzie was now attending Sunday morning activities only because it was a family requirement.

Other than hearing a few debates with her boyfriend, James, about Islam, which seemed like two young people arguing over philosophies, the subject had seemed to be dropped until she made the request to buy a Koran. The wind had shifted, but we didn't know that yet.

Stephanie and I respected Mack's request to compare the religions. We knew that once our daughter had something in her head we couldn't deter her, and we agreed that it was an encouraging sign that she came to me first. In our hearts, we believed there was no way a girl raised in an active Christian home could ever come to any other conclusion than that the Bible offered the Truth and the Koran did not. I never would have expected another outcome, but I also didn't know the real story behind her request. So I offered my Study Bible and commentaries, and I asked her to come to me with any questions during her comparison study.

The summer of 2013 was filled with our usual outdoor activities: going water-skiing, visiting our cabin, seeing new movies, playing video games, and cooking out. As the summer progressed, however, Mack surprised us by saying she wanted to break up with James. Mack said they had been having some problems for a while, and we decided to leave it at that.

Privately, Stephanie suspected there was more to it than what Mack was saying. Stephanie said to me, "If there was someone else, or an actual reason she didn't want to be with him anymore, that would make sense."

"They're teenagers. What makes sense at that age?" I asked with a shrug.

But I was surprised with how entrenched Mack was in her study of the Bible and the Koran. I still had no doubt that such a comparison would yield one, and only one, result: that Christianity was the clear and only option.

At first I admired Mack's dedication, but soon we realized that she was spending less time with her friends. By August, Mack had changed her eating habits. Our daughter's appetite was long a source of good family humor because it was short on nutritional balance and long on "this is what I really like." But suddenly she stopped eating bacon and sausage, for "healthy eating" reasons. Stephanie noticed Mack wearing jeans more and shorts less, highly unusual for her or anyone in the stifling August heat in Texas. She worked more hours at her job, and we didn't see her hanging out with anyone except on rare occasions.

With the start of her senior year of high school looming, only months after everything looked on target for an excellent year ahead, we had real concerns. Our happy Mackenzie was acting differently. She was aloof and lacked her usual excitement. She'd always talked about her senior year with high anticipation, but now that enthusiasm was gone. Her Koran–Bible comparison and our discussions about it also took a turn. She'd shifted from her curious study to a criticism of the faith she'd been raised in. Most alarming, her positions in our discussions on Islam and Christianity began swinging more and more toward the Islamic point of view.

To learn more about the religion, Stephanie signed up for a local class that taught about Islam and Muslim culture. I dug deeper into the Word. We both hoped this was only a short phase, and we prayed that our daughter would discover the truth quickly and be our Mack again—but with a stronger foundation in her faith.

Our happy Mackenzie was acting differently. She was aloof and lacked her usual excitement.

However, it was about to get a whole lot worse. And I could never have guessed what was really going on.

CHAPTER 3

Safety Nets

John

By the time Mackenzie reached high school, Stephanie and I were conditioned to look for signs of trouble with her. Stephanie usually detected them before I did. A shift in the tone of Mack's voice, the wording of a question, the phrasing of an answer, the timing of events, these were all signals to Stephanie that something was up. And Stephanie usually had a pretty good read on our daughter. When Mack went through her rebellious stage in middle school, I'd tell Stephanie she was seeing things that weren't there, but more often than not, Steph's instincts were dead-on.

I'd been exceptionally close to our daughter, and perhaps I wanted to give her the benefit of the doubt. Mackenzie and I enjoyed a unique relationship, and I was an involved dad from diapers to driving. When Mack was a baby, our morning tradition was for me to push her in her stroller around the neighborhood before I left for work, talking to her the entire way. As a dad, these were the greatest times. My little girl was totally innocent and trusting, absorbing everything around her. In the springtime, I'd point out the birds singing and I liked telling her it was "God's music," and then we'd stop and listen for a few minutes. I was totally infatuated with her and everybody knew it.

As Mack got older, she realized that on certain things Dad was the soft touch. I couldn't stand to hear her cry, and she had a practice of putting on quite a show for me at bedtime. Against the advice of my more insightful wife, when I'd hear her crying after we tucked her in, I'd always go back upstairs to check on her. After an extra thirty or forty-five minutes upstairs reading a second (and probably third) story, I'd sheepishly trudge back downstairs to Stephanie, who'd greet me with a shaking head and ask, "Why do you always fall for that?" I couldn't help it. She was my little girl.

I took Mack with me everywhere I went. I'd take my four-year-old daughter to the store with me, and inevitably when we'd get to the checkout counter she'd want a little something extra. I'd usually start by telling her "Not this time." But then she'd give me her "puppy dog look"—where she'd tilt her eyes up and lift her little hands like a puppy standing on two hind legs, pursing her lower lip out. About 99 percent of the time I would give in and get her what she wanted. When we walked into the house from the store, Mackenzie would be happily licking another ring pop, and Stephanie would give me a punitive look. I'd simply tell her, "Well, she just explains things better to me," and keep on walking.

One of the most difficult things we had to do was have Mackenzie attend daycare during her toddler years. Stephanie had a career of her own, and our families were in Louisiana while we were living in Dallas, so each of our kids attended daycare during our work hours. To be honest, putting Mack in daycare was probably harder on us than it was on her. We took her in late and picked her up early most days. The daycare we selected had a Christian foundation, good teachers, and a warm and friendly environment. Leaving her there was still extremely difficult, but it got a little easier for me after one memorable day when Mack was about five years old. I dropped Mack off in her classroom at eight o'clock that morning, and she was particularly clingy that day. She cried and cried and asked me not to leave. I stayed for a while and tried to explain to her that I had to go to work, but she wouldn't let go. After a good thirty or forty minutes, I reluctantly had to leave her crying in the room. I was walking down the hall when the school director pulled me aside. "Hey, John, I want you to take a look at something," she said. "Follow me." We went into her office, where there was a large bank of monitors with video feeds from each classroom.

"Take a look," the director told me.

She pointed to the monitor from Mackenzie's room, and I searched for the crying daughter I'd left a minute earlier. Instead, I found her happily playing at a table without a care in the world. The director smiled at me and said, "She does that every time, Dad. It's pretty much a big show she's putting on for you. She's fine." Chuckling and feeling much better, I thanked her and left for work. The next morning, I dropped Mack off at eight o'clock and she was again very clingy and her tears started flowing. This time I dropped to my knees in front of her and waved my index finger back and forth. I gently told her, "Uh-uh, not today! I'm on to your little game. I saw yesterday that as soon as I walk out the door you start playing. Now go over there with your friends, and I'll see you this afternoon." Mack gave me a big hug and said, "Okay, bye, Daddy!"

It didn't take long to see Mackenzie was going to be an active and unconventional kid. At a very young age, Mack fell in love with martial arts. At ten, she was ready to test for her black belt with Little Tigers Martial Arts. In this particular school, the test was quite unique and stands out as an example of the kind of spirit and tenacity Mackenzie possessed. Barefoot and dressed in a black gi and a wide brown belt, Mack looked across the blue mat at her opponent, a larger twelve-year-old boy wearing a black belt. The instructor screamed, "Go!" Mack, moving with surprising quickness, locked her arms under the boy's left arm, and then, spinning behind him, hooked her free hand under his right arm. All of a sudden the boy came flying over her knee as she slammed him to the mat. The instructor counted to three and then declared Mack the winner! Mackenzie jumped up and moved back to her corner for the second round.

> Barefoot and dressed in a black gi and a wide brown belt, Mack looked across the blue mat at her opponent, a larger twelve-year-old boy.

Her opponent, a little embarrassed and armed with a smidge more respect for the small-framed girl, moved back for round two. He threw Mackenzie to the mat, but she bounced back to her feet. A few seconds later, he threw her to the mat and was on top of her stomach. She didn't seem to be fighting back, and I couldn't understand what she was doing. Then I heard Mack calmly say to her opponent, "You're getting comfortable up there, aren't you? You won't be up there for long." Then Mack suddenly recoiled and bucked the boy completely off of her. Scrambling like a cat, she quickly pinned the black belt a second time. Mack shook her opponent's hand and sat in a waiting chair, exhausted but victorious. The Little Tigers black belt had been earned.

Now, Mackenzie, from her youngest age, was headstrong. Communication was typically very easy when you were in agreement with her, but it could get a bit (umph!) difficult when you were not. Stephanie and I certainly saw this at home, but High Adventure Treks had a way of putting you in situations where you had to confront and deal with adversity in different ways. One of our earliest adventures with HATS was loading a canoe with equipment and paddling about twelve miles down the Brazos River for an overnight camping trip with a dozen other father-daughter teams. The only problem was that Mackenzie, who was in sixth grade at the time, and I were not in the program when they taught how to actually handle the canoe! We also learned that day that in HATS a canoe isn't really a canoe. It's actually a seventeen-foot-long communication device. Experienced canoeists know that a canoe can only be steered from the rear, and in normal HATS tradition the daughter is stationed at the rear and Dad is put up front to paddle. As we crossed left and right and left and right and left and right, Mackenzie's frustration rose, which raised my frustration, which resulted in a rather animated discussion about who was actually steering the canoe and, well . . . I think you get the picture. When we mercifully reached the sandbar where we were spending the night, we were barely speaking to each other. That night, as things calmed down, I pulled out a deck of cards for our traditional game of War, and then we settled down side by side in our tent and fell asleep. The next morning, after some games and other activities, I was given a tiny orange piece of cord tied in a "friendship knot." Mackenzie had one that was yellow. We were asked to exchange them and tell each other something we admired about the other person. We enjoyed a special time on that sandbar in the middle of nowhere. Later, when we repacked the canoe, Mack took her place at the rear and I settled in at the front, and we directed our "communication device" straight as an arrow to the pickup point.

As parents, Stephanie and I placed a premium on the time we spent with our kids. We spent as much time as possible at our family cabin in southeast Oklahoma, and we took the kids tubing, knee-boarding, wakeboarding, and swimming at the lakes around Dallas/ Fort Worth. In the fall, we'd take them horseback riding and hiking.

There were few things our kids loved to do more. We often invited many of Mack's friends out for the day with us, not only for their enjoyment, but also so we could get to know them better.

In her middle school years, Mackenzie was very interested in marine mammals, particularly orcas. In those preteen years, she attended a few SeaWorld camps in the summer and set her young eyes on becoming a trainer. We embraced her dreams, not so much because we wanted her swimming around a tank with a top-shelf ocean predator, but because we believed it would encourage her in many areas she would love—swimming, scuba diving, and biology. Her love of killer whales stayed strong and she studied everything she could find on them.

Before long, Mackenzie knew exactly what was required to one day work with the orcas. She joined a swim club at age thirteen to ensure she could pass the rigorous swim test. She even practiced holding her breath so she could pass the underwater test. We gave Mack one of our biggest surprises for her when she returned from a weeklong SeaWorld camp. While she was gone, we arranged for a friend to redecorate her room into an ocean theme, complete with a hand-painted oil on canvas of the iconic orca tail slipping into the water, with the SeaWorld theme "Believe" painted across the top in its recognizable script. Mack was awestruck when she returned home and walked into her room.

Stephanie and I took every precaution to make sure our daughter was safe. When Mack was in elementary school, she started asking us for a cell phone of her own. We made her wait until the sixth grade and then gave her a phone that texted but didn't have access to the Internet and other applications. We thought she needed one because she was participating in so many after-school activities. Many of Mack's friends had received phones long before her, and she didn't get a smartphone until her freshman year of high school.

Early on, we periodically checked her text messages, but we were admittedly not as diligent as we should have been once she was older.

We had the typical parental controls on the computers our children had access to, and we occasionally checked the browsing history to make sure they weren't accessing inappropriate websites. Our kids were not allowed to take laptops upstairs or into their bedrooms. In fact, Mack wasn't allowed to take a computer into her bedroom until her senior year, when she needed to use it for homework. She was eighteen years old and would be leaving home soon, and she had earned our trust by having a good junior year.

We talked to Mack, Luke, and Michael a lot about the appropriate use of computers and phones. We told Mack not to answer calls from numbers she didn't recognize and to only give her number to friends. She had to have our permission to start Facebook, Instagram, and email accounts. We had multiple conversations with her about not accepting Facebook invites from people she didn't know, and on at least two occasions we had her go through her friends list and eliminate anyone she couldn't tell us about. We discussed the dangers of Internet chat rooms and told her to be careful about responding to people she didn't know. Safety on social media was a regular point of discussion in her school as well.

> We discussed the dangers of Internet chat rooms and told her to be careful about responding to people she didn't know.

When Mack first started showing an interest in dating during her freshman year, we did not allow her to have "car dates." We drove her to meet her date at a restaurant or movie and then picked her up afterward. I made a point of meeting the boys and talking to them in order to size them up. She wasn't allowed to ride with a boy to a date until the latter part of her sophomore year, and only after the young man came to our door so we could meet him. Mack typically dated boys from her school, so there was never an issue with her dating young men who were older. Stephanie and I talked to her regularly about dating and relationships.

Stephanie and I had taken an active role in our children's lives, and we thought we'd done everything we could to educate them about the dangers of the Internet and social media. Mackenzie was about to become a high school senior and was becoming more and more independent, and she seemed to take our advice to heart. We often reminded her, "Anybody can be anything for a little while. Time will tell who they really are." Unfortunately, we were about to find out the true meaning of that statement.

CHAPTER 4

A Harmless Meeting

Mackenzie

It started pretty innocently.

One night in April 2013, my best friend, Madison, and I were hanging out at her house, like we often did since becoming inseparable our sophomore year of high school. After having dinner with her parents, we headed up to her room, where I fell back on her bed and sent off a text to my boyfriend.

"Hey, let's get on Omegle," Madison said as she pulled out her laptop.

When Madison first showed me the social media site, I liked it because it was unpredictable and had an unusual concept. The website offered a "chat roulette" with people from around the world. Omegle randomly connected people, giving them the opportunity to either have a conversation through video chat (like Skype) or just be able to see the other person and type messages back and forth. Madison and I liked how easy it was to move on from people and how they could move on from us. If we decided we weren't interested in someone, we simply clicked the "next" button, and a new person popped up.

The site's tagline, *Talk to Strangers!*, sounded like fun, and though I'd grown up like all of my peers with parents and adults saying "Don't talk to strangers," this seemed different. We were talking to people from the safety and privacy of our own homes. They didn't know where we were and they couldn't find out. It wasn't like we were meeting them for real. Besides, we had all the control to swipe past anyone we didn't like, and no personal information was shared. Nothing bad could happen, or so I thought.

"I don't know," I said, looking at my phone. I wasn't really in the mood to go on Omegle. Truth was, after the initial intrigue, I had quickly found it to be a little dumb.

"What else are we going to do?" Madison said, and she had a point.

"Okay, why not?" I said as Madison logged in from her desk across the room.

I pulled a chair up beside Madison and watched over her shoulder as Omegle randomly threw male profiles at us like an online version of *The Bachelorette*.

"No, not him," I said, laughing.

Madison kept hitting "next" as we'd lean in to see the guys. Sometimes she would type back and forth for a short time, and then we'd be on to the next one. Most of the guys were nothing special. A few of them seemed nice at first, but soon began asking suggestive questions or making inappropriate requests.

"You girls are really beautiful," one guy typed, but Madison quickly passed on to another guy.

Another one leaned forward and said, "Wow, niiiice! You girls want to—"

"Next," Madison said with a grin.

"Hey, there," said a guy who looked too old to be on the site.

As Madison hit "next," we joked about how the guy probably lived in his mom's basement. After a while, I went back to my phone while Madison remained on the site. We sometimes typed back and forth with a few guys, but mostly we observed the people and enjoyed the summer evening.

Madison had been online for a while when she hopped up.

"Come, take my spot. I gotta run to the bathroom."

I sat in the warm chair at her desk and started scrolling through people when a guy popped up who was very good-looking. He had chiseled features like a model, and I couldn't help wanting to look at him a bit longer.

"Hello, how are you doing today?" he wrote.

"I'm good. How are you?"

"I am very good."

I waited for him to turn creepy and say something inappropriate, but he was nice and friendly the whole time, which made him stand out.

> He had chiseled features like a model, and I couldn't help wanting to look at him a bit longer.

"Where are you from?" I typed.

"New York."

"That's cool." This made him less foreign and more relatable.

"What about you?"

"I'm in Texas, have you ever been here?" I knew not to be specific about locations on these sites.

"No, I have not, but would like to."

His name was Aadam, and he was outgoing and fun to talk to without being too forward or pushy, which most of the other guys on the website were within the first ten minutes.

"Did you find someone?" Madison asked when she returned. "Wow, he's cute!"

"I know, right?"

If I could build my ideal guy, he would look a lot like Aadam. His eyes were a darker blue, almost gray depending on the light. I've never been too crazy about blue eyes, but his were intense and intriguing. He had a strong jawline outlined with a short trimmed scruff. His brown hair was a little on the longer side, but not too long and nicely brushed back to the right. He had a light complexion and, based on the way he was dressed, I would have guessed he was from Europe or even America. When he smiled, his teeth were white and looked practically perfect. He looked at me with a sheepish grin, as if he didn't know how attractive he was. From his broad shoulders and toned look, he definitely worked out often. No doubt he would make any girl who saw him want to stop and admire him.

We switched seats, and Madison continued the conversation.

He messaged with her for a little while and then wrote, "Where did the other girl go?"

Madison gave me a grin.

"He likes you, not me."

"And I have a boyfriend," I said.

I leaned over and saw the guy again. "Well, what's the harm? We're just talking."

"Exactly."

Since Madison had been on the site for a while already, she didn't mind me taking over, so I continued to chat with Aadam for another two hours until my curfew was approaching.

"I need to go," I typed.

"Well, it was very good talking."

"Yes, it was." I didn't want to go, suddenly. I wondered if I'd see Aadam on the website again. He seemed reluctant to leave too.

"Do you have a Facebook page? We can connect there and

sometimes talk if you want," he wrote. His small grin was incredibly charming.

"Sure, that sounds good."

It was at that point he wrote, "Now do not judge me, but I am Muslim."

I assumed he let me know this so I wouldn't be surprised when I saw it on his Facebook page. But it didn't bother me, and I actually thought it was sweet that he was worried about it. He didn't look anything like most of the Muslim guys I knew in high school, and he definitely didn't look like the Islamic extremists I'd seen on TV. He was dressed well in quality jeans and a T-shirt that fit snugly around his biceps.

He sent a friend request to me on Facebook, and I accepted it. The next morning, I woke to a message from Aadam. I was surprised to hear back from him so quickly. There was still a lot I didn't know about him, so I scrolled through his photos on Facebook before needing to get ready for school. Our conversation the night before had lasted several hours. It was fun chatting with him, and he acted genuinely interested in me. He didn't say or act inappropriately either. Everything pointed toward him being a decent guy. There were no red flags, and it seemed like a harmless new friendship.

I messaged him back before leaving for school and hoped I'd hear from him soon. It was a beginning, and I never could have imagined where this meeting would take my

> I never could have guessed that this person could pull me in and manipulate my thoughts of myself, my culture, and even my God.

family and me. I never could have guessed that my entire life was about to change, and that independent me could get sucked into a vacuum of lies and untruths. I never could have guessed that this person could pull me in and manipulate my thoughts of myself, my culture, and even my God.

At this moment, it all just seemed new and exciting. What could go wrong with that?

CHAPTER 5

Growing Attachments

Mackenzie

After meeting Aadam on Omegle and accepting his Facebook friend request, I continued to chat online with him over the next few weeks. Based on the photographs he shared on Facebook, it didn't seem like he actually lived in New York. When I asked Aadam if he really lived there, he admitted that he was actually from Kosovo in the Balkan region of Europe.

The fact that he had lied to me about where he lived should have been an immediate red flag, but I wasn't too concerned about it. We were nothing more than acquaintances at that point, and I was fascinated that he lived such a unique and different life from mine in the United States. I wanted to learn more about him and where he lived. Initially, it was more like we were pen pals, and that's really what our relationship was for a while. We messaged each other on Facebook and made small talk in the beginning. Then, as we became more familiar and comfortable with each other, we shared details about our lives, such as our future plans, hopes and dreams, and even stories about our families. Our conversations were fun and enjoyable. Because we felt so comfortable communicating with each other, after only a few weeks it seemed I'd known him forever.

After several weeks, I suggested we use Skype to communicate, since we hadn't seen each other on video since that first night we met on Omegle. It was nice to see him. It made him so real. He was just as I remembered. His dark blue eyes looked compassionate and excited. He nervously fixed his hair and gave me a half smile. He was wearing a navy-blue button-down, and he had a leather bracelet on his left wrist, which looked worn, as if he'd had it for a long time. I smiled back at him and waved.

Once we started using Skype, the frequency of our conversations increased dramatically. I'd get out of school at one thirty every afternoon, and I'd have a couple of hours to kill before I went to work. Since Kosovo was seven hours ahead of Dallas, Aadam was already home from school and had finished his chores. We'd Skype every day on my laptop between my classes and work. I'd still hang out with my friends, and I talked with him whenever I could. Honestly, things were fine at that point, and it was like I'd met a new friend who lived on the other side of the world.

Although we were now video-chatting, Aadam never spoke and only typed words to me.

Although we were now video-chatting, Aadam never spoke and we only typed words to each other. I could see his handsome face, read his facial expressions, and hear his laugh, but he never communicated to me with spoken words. It was odd and frustrating at first, but after a while it became kind of normal. Still, I desperately wanted him to say something to me so I could hear his voice, but he'd make the excuse that his English wasn't very good and he was self-conscious about it. Albanian, Serbian, and Turkish are the native languages in Kosovo, and very few people there speak English. I have to admit Aadam's humility was attractive.

Eventually it reached the point where I was eagerly waiting for Aadam's messages and so looking forward to our conversations. I found myself thinking of him throughout the day, and often I wanted to talk to him more than anything else, even more than spending time with my family and friends and being with my boyfriend. Aadam and I had developed a connection. I knew a lot about him and his family, and he knew intimate details about mine. At that point, I still would have defined our relationship as a friendship, but, given my intense desire to talk to him, I knew it was probably growing into something more. I didn't want to admit to anyone, including myself, that I might have a romantic interest in him. As we continued to talk more and more over the next several weeks, I could tell my feelings were growing stronger.

But the language barrier was still a big obstacle for me. Aadam and I had only been talking by typing at this point. He could write English fairly well, but he said he couldn't speak it very well. He told me it was much easier for him to type because it gave him more time to translate from his original language, Albanian, to English. He said when he tried to speak English, he would sometimes forget words and get nervous and confused, so he just stuck to using the keyboard. He felt more comfortable that way. I was patient and I understood his reservations, but I was growing tired of not hearing his voice. Finally, I told him I wanted him to speak to me, and I would help him learn to speak English. It started with me typing words as I spoke them so he could hear the English words. The first thing Aadam said to me was his name. He had a very cute accent, and it was nice to finally hear him talk. It made him even more real to me.

At first he wouldn't speak often, only every now and then. He would send me five-second videos, such as a message saying "Good morning!" When we tried to have conversations in English, he would say something and mispronounce it, causing us to laugh together. There was probably a month of that kind of interaction, and helping him learn English made me feel special to him and needed.

Aadam was a very fast learner, maybe too fast, and I began to suspect that he might have known more English than he had initially let on. I remember the first night Aadam actually had a full conversation with me. My parents were home, and I didn't want them to know I was talking to anyone. Deep down, I knew I shouldn't be talking to him so much. I already had a boyfriend.

> Aadam was a very fast learner, maybe too fast, and I began to suspect that he might have known more English than he had initially let on.

James and I had been dating about a year when things started to get shaky. Neither of us had dated anyone else as long as we'd been dating each other, and we were determined to try to make it work. He was and is a great guy. We became very close through tenth and eleventh grades. We had some exceptional times and memories, but I knew things were beginning to crumble. He signed a contract with the military that required him to serve at least four years after college. He was planning to go to a college out of state, and we would be separated. I was happy for him, but deep down I knew it was the first step of us growing apart. We tried to hang on to what we had, but in the end it wasn't enough. We ended up taking a break for several months, and finally officially broke up in late September. Aadam and I talked for several months before James and I officially ended it, but it's important to bring up that Aadam and I were only pen pals for a significant amount of time. I had a lot of respect for James and didn't take our relationship lightly. Toward the end of my relationship with James, I felt a desire to talk to Aadam even more. I knew I was starting to develop feelings for him, but I needed to deal with my current relationship before I even thought of Aadam romantically. After James and I decided we were better off apart, Aadam and I talked like we normally did, but I was feeling more drawn to him than before, and now nothing was stopping me from talking to him as much as I wanted.

I wouldn't say I broke up with James for Aadam, but he was an extra push—and perhaps even motivation—for me to do it. Once I was single, there wasn't much reason for me not to like Aadam. Since we had never met in person, I told myself I was only enjoying his company. In my heart, though, I knew I was beginning to feel very deep emotions for him. This was only the first of many inner conflicts I would have about him.

After I broke up with James, my relationship with Aadam only intensified. Over the next three months he sent me a Facebook message every morning and then he would ask me to message him before I went to sleep so he would know I was safe in bed. Looking back, I can see how that was his subtle way of controlling me, but I thought it was sweet at the time. Sometimes he'd message me at two o'clock in the morning because he couldn't sleep. I always had my phone near me so I would be there when he needed me.

Eventually I found out that if you have a cell phone without a carrier SIM card, you could make phone calls and send text messages over Facebook and Skype without it being tracked on a data plan. Aadam didn't have a phone, so I mailed him my old iPhone, which enabled us to talk more easily and more often when he had access to Wi-Fi but didn't have his laptop with him. We mostly talked while I was at school so I could use the Wi-Fi there, which prevented my parents from knowing I was on Facebook so much. Once he had a phone, things became even more personal between us. Our conversations became so frequent that I was even video-chatting with him during lunch. Our conversations went on for hours. We discussed anything; it didn't really matter to me. Using the phone, he would FaceTime me while at his college or a coffee bar. I now didn't just see him in his room, so he became more real to me.

Our frequent conversations and growing familiarity made me feel very close to him. At night, I would lay down and talk to him. In the complete dark, hearing just his voice, it was easy to forget he was across the world. It felt so normal. Often he would need to go to sleep, but we couldn't stop talking. It would be eight P.M. in Dallas, but three A.M. in Kosovo. I could tell he was so tired and would encourage him to sleep, but he wouldn't hang up. He just kept asking me questions. I'd smile and we'd continue to talk. When we were video-chatting, I'd look into his eyes, and it was like daydreaming. Time would fly as we talked. A three-hour conversation seemed like thirty minutes. I truly believed I was special to him.

One time, Aadam was about to go out with some friends and asked me to help him pick out what to wear. (I was slightly flattered, because I thought his style sense was better than mine.) He held up a black-striped shirt. I shook my head no. He then picked out a blue button-down. I liked it but asked him to try it on first. He slipped it on over his undershirt for me to see. The shirt was nice, but I said no again. He laughed, took off the shirt, and threw it at the camera on his computer. He then picked out a black button-down, which I had him try on. I loved it. Something about the shirt was clean and strong-looking, like a gentleman would wear. I told him that shirt was the one. He laughed and called me crazy.

Those were the moments I loved him sharing with me. I was beginning to wonder if this could actually be real for us.

CHAPTER 6

Making Plans

Mackenzie

Aadam told me he lived with his brother, parents, and grandmother on a small family farm on the outskirts of a moderately sized town in Kosovo. Rolling hills, trees, and fields surrounded the farm, where they raised goats and chickens. Every morning a rooster crowed and woke Aadam up, and it became a running joke between us that the rooster was the family alarm clock.

During one of our early Skype conversations, Aadam showed me his backyard, which was very pretty. He was standing on a hill, and I could see the hills in the distance and a farm about twenty yards away. There were neighboring houses, but none were very close. The porch of his house was a rusty color, and there were chimes that made a beautiful noise whenever the wind blew. I could hear the rooster in the distance, and I could barely make out the shape of goats behind the chickens.

Aadam was very proud of his brother, Omar, who was five years older and recently married. In a lot of ways, it seemed that Aadam strived to be exactly like his brother. He loved the idea of having a family and a reliable job. But Aadam said his dream seemed unattainable because there were very few good jobs in Kosovo. He did seem to be intelligent and said he attended a nearby university, but Aadam rarely talked about his schoolwork, other than the occasional test or assignment. In the absence of a job, he helped his family around the farm, cleaning dishes, sweeping, feeding animals, and collecting eggs.

Aadam and I first talked about meeting each other in person in the initial weeks after we began talking to each other. Since we were sort of pen pals, it sounded fun to be able to grab coffee with someone from somewhere so foreign to me. Aadam had plans to visit the United States in about a year, so if we were still in contact, he said he would make a stop in Dallas to meet me.

When he originally proposed this idea, I didn't actually believe it would happen. In all honesty, I figured we wouldn't be talking in two weeks, let alone a year from then, and that we would eventually forget about each other. As I listened to his travel plans, I smiled and nodded my head in agreement. What was the point in telling him I didn't think we would get that far? I simply said, "Let's just see where we are in a year." Aadam didn't push it at first, so we'd quickly move on to our next topic of conversation.

> Aadam and I first talked about meeting each other in person in the initial weeks after we began talking to each other.

As the summer of 2013 began, I found myself actually hoping we would get the chance to meet. He didn't bring it up often, but when he did, I was excited at the thought of him coming to the United States. Pretty soon I was even contributing to the plans of him coming to see me. I told him about good airports and easy ways to travel. But after about two months of us making plans for him to come to Dallas, Aadam told me he would not have enough money to travel that far south. Aadam said he would only be able to fly to New York, and I would have to go there if we wanted to meet. I didn't think there was any way I could convince my parents to let me travel to New York by myself, and so I was resigned to the fact that I'd probably never get to meet him. When Aadam asked me if I thought it was a possibility, I responded, "I have to see. Maybe I can."

In the back of my mind, I still felt like it would probably be a moot point because we would eventually stop talking. Surely we couldn't keep up our conversations until next summer! After we said good night, I closed my laptop. I sank down into my chair feeling a bit deflated. I hadn't realized how much I was looking forward to meeting Aadam until then. Several times after that, he brought up the possibility of meeting me in New York. He sent me information about airline ticket prices and fun tourist activities we could do together. It really did seem like it would be a lot of fun. As I did more research about going to New York, I became more excited about the possibility—not just of seeing Aadam, but also in doing something so different. Eventually Aadam told me he was planning on staying in New York for three months, and he wanted me to come visit for a few days. I told him I would try to make it work. I wasn't sure it would happen, but that was my plan.

By this point Aadam and I had become so connected that I felt like our friendship wasn't something I could easily back out of. That's about the time he started talking to me about his religion. It was obvious to me that Aadam's faith was important to him. He would say things like, "I really shouldn't talk to you because I'm Muslim." Or he would nonchalantly say, "I can't talk to a girl I'm not engaged with." Initially, his comments bothered me a little, but I simply changed the subject and moved on. As we grew closer, he asked questions about my faith. Often, I didn't have answers for him, despite being raised in the church and attending services nearly every Sunday. As I grew closer to Aadam, I became focused on learning more about Islam. That's when I decided to ask my dad if I could purchase a Koran to learn more about Aadam's religion. At the time, I had no idea where that request would lead me.

Aadam would nonchalantly say, "I can't talk to a girl I'm not engaged with."

The Islam that Aadam talked about sounded respectable and intriguing. During our phone calls or Skype sessions, he'd often leave for five minutes to pray. He prayed five times a day, always at the same time. I respected his deep commitment to his faith. It was refreshing to see someone with that much dedication to doing what he believed was right. It was also a relief for me to find someone who didn't make inappropriate requests, like many guys do. During the entire year we talked, Aadam never asked me for anything inappropriate, not even photos, and he was always respectful. I also never sent or wrote anything inappropriate. It all just felt so honest and harmless.

CHAPTER 7

Examining Faith

John

When Mackenzie asked to purchase a Koran so she could compare it to the Bible, her unusual request gave me pause, and I did not take it lightly. I knew Mack had many facets to her personality, but having an intellectual curiosity about spiritual matters was not one of them. However, I tried to view it as an opportunity.

Stephanie and I have always taught our kids that they need to understand why they believe what they believe. I have held firm to the conviction that analyzing the Bible—whether it is through science, another religion, or self-reflection—is not a bad thing as long as you are responsible in how you do it. Against the backdrop of today's pluralistic society and modern science, it is disingenuous for Christians to give overly simplistic responses to difficult questions. Christ, the Bible, and Christianity have withstood challenges for more than two thousand years, and they are perfectly capable of standing up to anything that anyone can throw at them, as long as we are fair and responsible in how we defend them. Living by faith doesn't mean you cannot ask questions or allow yourself to be exposed to other lines of reasoning. If done honestly and respectfully, I believe it can be a method of growing spiritually.

From my experience, spiritual awakening often occurs during the late teens and early adulthood. Young people like Mack, who were raised in the church and who accepted Christ as Savior at an early age, might begin to question their beliefs once they're older. It's a natural progression, and it's not the same journey for everyone. So when Mackenzie asked me about buying a Koran when she was nearly eighteen, my interpretation was that it was the beginning of that quest for her. Researching Islam is certainly not the way I thought her spiritual journey would begin, but in the end, I felt she was probably wondering why the Bible was so central to our family and our beliefs. To me, it was a tremendous opportunity for her to see the depth and wonder of the Scripture. I cautioned Mack that doing a comparison of Christianity and Islam was not easy. The Bible is not written like a novel. It dips and dives in time and thought. Spiritual insights come in layers; even the teachings of Jesus are multifaceted. Scripture should not be taken out of context; nearly all events, teachings, and people in biblical history intertwine with each other to create the full picture. This is why you can find fresh insights that inspire and enlighten when you study the Scripture over and over.

As Mackenzie started what I hoped would be an enlightened examination of her faith, I asked her to come to me with any questions she had, and I promised to either help her myself or find someone who could. I provided her with my New International Version (NIV) Study Bible, some good commentaries, and my ideas on a blueprint of how she should frame her study. Against this tapestry, I agreed that she could buy a Koran and start her journey.

To say I was fully confident that it was the right thing to do would be a serious understatement. It was a judgment call, but I had an underlying confidence that Christ would lead us. Nonetheless, it is a decision I've second-guessed many times since. Stephanie tells me that regardless of how I answered her request that day, Mackenzie was going to do what she was going to do.

> **As Mackenzie started what I hoped would be an enlightened examination of her faith, I asked her to come to me with any questions.**

But it never occurred to me that Mackenzie could read the Bible—something she had heard her entire life—compare it to what is written in the Koran, and then lean toward the Koran. Unfortunately, I was wrong. Additionally, and perhaps most important, if Mack's motives that day had been purely spiritual in nature, it might have turned out differently. Months later we would learn that wasn't the case.

Mackenzie began her study with enthusiasm. She purchased a small paperback Koran and a faux-leather journal to keep notes. She explained to me in detail how she was going to read a chapter in the Koran and a chapter in the Bible and then planned to take diligent notes. I encouraged her to begin in the New Testament, probably with the book of John, as her starting point in the Bible. She took careful notes and asked me to read a few of her thoughts. At first she came to me with questions about the Bible and what certain passages meant. I gladly explained the biblical perspective and offered additional verses for her to use for context. Before long, she had several pages of careful handwritten notes—one side the Koran and on the other side, the Bible. I figured her comparison would run for a few weeks and then she would grow bored with the time it required. But, much to my surprise, she persisted in her study.

Mackenzie

People who are passionate about something are inspiring. They have this fire in their eyes when they talk about their passion, and you can tell that it means the world to them that you are taking the time to listen to their heart on whatever subject it happens to be. That is how it was with Aadam and Islam. He could talk for hours upon hours, and he was just happy that I was listening to him.

At first Aadam talking about Islam annoyed me a bit, only because it was foreign to me and I was a Christian. But as he dove deeper into the differences between his religion and mine, I found that I didn't have much biblical knowledge to defend my Christian faith. But I reiterated what little I could remember from Bible studies and youth groups, even if it didn't carry much weight against what he was telling me. It worked for a while, but eventually his questions became more difficult to answer and harder to research on Google.

When Aadam challenged Christianity in a way that I was not able to defend, he would then send me links to videos on the Internet that he said disproved what was written in the Bible. Then he would read from the Koran to fill in what he said were gaps. Our conversations went on like this for a month or so. Eventually, at Aadam's urging, I decided to try and compare the Bible to the Koran.

My plan was to honestly compare what was written about specific topics in both the Bible and the Koran. My approach went okay

> He sent me links to videos that he said disproved what was written in the Bible. Then he would read from the Koran to fill in what he said were gaps.

for a while, but soon Aadam was bombarding me with videos and other information about Islam. At one point, he compared Christian girls to Muslim girls. "Look around!" he told me. "The proof of what is the right religion is all around you!" He told me that Muslim girls don't stray far from the Koran because it is the right religion, but Christian girls go in every direction. I have to admit, he had a point. Many girls I knew claimed to be Christian, yet they went out and partied or hooked up with every guy they met. The more I thought about what he said, the more it bothered me.

Aadam also sent me videos of priests and imams debating religion, and the imam would "stun" the priest, or make a point that sounded like he was correct. Before too long, I became consumed by the videos and filled my head with what the imams were saying. Eventually I realized I was no longer comparing the Bible to the Koran and was simply studying the Koran.

As my study progressed, Aadam told me to ask my parents questions about religion. When my parents became defensive, Aadam told me they were only upset because they didn't know what to say and had been proven wrong. (This was not the case, but I didn't know any better at the time.) My discussions with my parents became more heated, and the wedge between us became larger and larger. Of course, when I was upset after a fight with my mom and dad, Aadam was right there to pick me up and encourage me. Before the end of the summer, it was a routine cycle of destruction in our house, and Aadam was becoming the only person I believed.

One day I sat down on my bed and started a normal conversation with Aadam. I showed him a few lower-priced flight options to New York I'd found for him, as well as a few hotels where he could stay. He seemed sort of disinterested and wasn't contributing much to the conversation.

After a little while, I asked Aadam what was bothering him. He didn't want to tell me at first, but after about ten minutes he reluctantly admitted he couldn't come to the United States. I was crushed and couldn't believe what I was hearing. After talking to him for four months, I really had my heart set on meeting him.

"Why not?" I asked, while trying not to sound too panicked.

Aadam told me he wouldn't have enough money to make the trip. The airline tickets were expensive enough, but the hotels were even more costly. He didn't have a job, so he was trying to scrape together whatever money he could and was going to be short.

We continued to try to come up with ideas to make it cheaper for him, but we couldn't think of anything. After we said good night, I sat in my room thinking. I wanted to see him so badly, especially after everything we'd been through the past few months.

I had the idea to look up how much it would cost for Aadam to travel to Switzerland, since I was going there anyway the summer after I graduated. It was an eighteen-hour drive from Kosovo to Switzerland, so maybe it would be a good meeting point. I figured I could take my amazing graduation trip to Switzerland, and Aadam could meet me there. He was overjoyed when I brought up this idea. He said a train ride to Switzerland wouldn't be too expensive for him, and if I could buy a one-way ticket, I could even stay with him a little longer and it would be cheaper. But I knew it would be hard to explain to my parents why I wanted a one-way ticket, so if we had to spend more money on a two-way, that's what we'd do to avoid raising suspicion.

In September 2013, during one of our Skype sessions, Aadam told me he had big news. His eyes were bright with excitement and he could barely sit still. He said his brother's wife was pregnant. I was so happy for Omar, but I found myself even more excited for Aadam. He had a huge smile and was laughing. Then I saw his brother walk behind him on the camera, and Aadam turned around and gave him a pat on his shoulder. At that point, his brother noticed me and offered me a friendly hello with a wave. I quickly responded, "Congratulations!" Omar looked a bit confused, and I realized he didn't understand English. Aadam laughed and translated what I said for him. That was my first contact with his family. It wasn't much, but it felt good.

CHAPTER 8

Twisting Scripture

John

As Mackenzie began her senior year at Plano West Senior High School in August 2013, Stephanie and I realized she wasn't hanging out with her old friends. We wondered if she'd become part of a new crowd, but then we realized she wasn't hanging out with hardly anyone. At the start of the summer, Mack was lined up for a memorable and happy senior year. Now it was evident it was going to be an unforgettable year, but for all the wrong reasons.

Mackenzie was working more hours at her job, coming home right before her curfew, and then leaving early the next morning for school. It was the same thing every day, and she was spending very little time with her brothers or us. Most alarming, Mack's positions in our discussions about Islam and Christianity began swinging more and more to the Islamic point of view. Throughout the summer, our religious discussions had turned into debates, debates into arguments, arguments into a defense of Islam, and ultimately an outright rejection of Christianity.

How could the daughter we raised in the church cast aside everything she'd been raised to believe in? She'd grown up in the church from the time she was six weeks old. She had wonderful Sunday school teachers, choir directors, and youth ministers. We couldn't have asked for a better church to nurture and support Mack as she grew up. But now something wasn't clicking with her when it came to Christianity, and she was exploring Islam. For the life of me, I couldn't understand why.

> Throughout the summer, our religious discussions had turned into debates, and debates into arguments.

When Mack first started her "comparison" of Christianity and Islam, she asked me about Jesus and how we, as Christians, could be so certain he was the Son of God. I discussed with her the fulfillment of prophecies laid out in the Old Testament, the miracles he performed and the theological meaning behind them, his teachings that have resonated with truth and wisdom through the ages, his example of love to all men, and the multilayered facets of his crucifixion and resurrection.

She asked me about the authenticity of the Bible and how it was translated. I explained to her that theologians have always been very honest about the fact that we do not have the very first manuscripts, but how we have many manuscripts preserved from throughout the ages that were studied, compared, and validated, proving how meticulously the biblical record was retained.

We discussed why there are different translations of the Bible, as well as the differences between a translation like the New International Version (NIV) and a paraphrase like the Message. To help her better understand, I offered to arrange for her to meet with one of the premier biblical editors in the United States, whom I was acquainted with, in order to answer her questions with a voice of authority. She was adamantly not interested in meeting him. At first my answers to her questions had been met with acceptance, but in a short period of time they were met with skepticism.

While I struggled to grasp what was happening with my daughter, the one positive I tried to keep in mind was that she was asking me questions that were actually about important concepts any Christian should understand. Mackenzie, in typical fashion, never takes the normal (or easy) route to anything. But we were hopeful that once she'd worked her way through her study, her Christian beliefs would be even stronger. Sadly, it didn't work out that way. Before long, our discussions about faith became more frequent, more contentious, much louder, and increasingly more from the Muslim point of view. The more we pushed Mackenzie, the more resistant to Christianity she seemed to get.

After a few weeks of study, Mackenzie began pointing out what she believed were conflicts and discrepancies in the biblical record. At first they were things we could handle, such as, "Why is Jesus called both the 'Son of God' and the 'Son of Man'?" Or why there were more than twelve disciples listed in the Scripture. But soon the questions swung sharply toward the classic Islamic arguments, such as the doctrine of the Trinity and how salvation could possibly come from grace.

As our debates with Mackenzie intensified, it was obvious to us that she was not getting her lines of thought from her own independent study. The mystery of her source of information was partially revealed when she asked me to watch an Islamic video with her. She told me the cleric could explain what she was telling me better than she could. At first I strongly resisted her request to watch. I had no interest in watching Islamic videos, and I maintained that stance for a while. For one thing, I didn't feel like I needed to hear or understand an Islamic cleric's issues with my religion. And I certainly didn't see any reason I needed to debate Mackenzie through the proxy of an anti-Christian video that she couldn't understand herself.

> As our debates with Mackenzie intensified, it was obvious to us that she was not getting her lines of thought from her own independent study.

Night after night Stephanie and I would go through these arguments with her, and over time Mack adopted a fully Islamic stance. We were crushed. Nothing we said, nothing we showed her, nothing we offered, made an iota of impact. It was like talking to a wall.

One night I went upstairs, where Mackenzie was sitting in the game room with her computer in her lap. I heard a distinct dialect that I believed was coming from one of the Islamic videos she wanted me to watch. Finally, I was fed up. I went downstairs and grabbed my Bible. Then I sat down next to her and told her to take me through the video. The Islamic cleric pointed out everything he believed was wrong with Christianity. Over and over again, he'd read a passage and then offer his comments on why it was wrong. Now, I'm no theologian, but I've studied the Bible enough to be comfortable with talking about a lot of it. I made her pause the video on every single point the cleric made. I'd take each argument he made, look up each verse from the Scripture, and I would read it in its full context and try to explain to her what it really meant.

For four grueling hours, until two o'clock in the morning, I went through the video point by point with her. Mackenzie was an unwilling participant and was furious, but it was important to me that if she insisted on using Islamic videos as her source of information, then she needed to know they were full of holes and inaccuracies.

Did I think my lecture would turn her back toward Christianity and Jesus? I hoped so, but if nothing else, I hoped it would break the veneer, or at least cast some doubt and teach her that you cannot take the opinion from one man on a video and throw out everything you were raised to trust.

Much to my dismay, my lecture didn't seem to have changed anything. I had hoped to make an impact, but Mack was unchanged by the revelations, and her doubts continued to grow. In fact, after that memorable night, our long hours of debate no longer remained confined to theology. We also started to argue about the cultural differences between Christians and Muslims. For the life of me, I couldn't understand why Mackenzie, who is naturally independent and stubborn, would want to go anywhere near a religion in which the role of women is so radically different from everything she knows. Stephanie and I were completely baffled.

Stephanie and I became increasingly frustrated. She and Mackenzie had a long tradition of watching a DVD of a crime series like *Bones* or *CSI* on most nights. As Mackenzie grew older, it was also the best time for Stephanie to talk with her about school, boys, and other problems. When Mack went through her rebellious stage during her freshman year of high school, it was not a very fun time for either one of them. However, this nightly ritual persisted even during the most difficult of times and was often the time when Mackenzie would be most open to talking about what was on her mind. Now their rare nights together were being heavily taxed as Mackenzie wrestled with Christianity and Islam. Their discussions typically started out quietly enough, but often would escalate into full-scale shouting matches, then, almost without fail, the anger would subside and they would calmly continue to talk. Not much progress was made from Stephanie's point of view, but at least the communication lines were still open.

Eventually Stephanie used those moments to challenge Mackenzie on why she was so interested in a religion whose views of a woman's role in the home was the polar opposite from how she was raised. Stephanie talked to her about what life would be like as a Muslim woman, and how she would have to be submissive to the men in her home. Stephanie asked Mack about her potential role in a Muslim household, including the expectation that she would be expected to carry the full load of housework and other chores. Of course, we knew that Mackenzie absolutely hated household chores! Stephanie also discussed with her how many Muslim women are required to dress quite modestly and many of them are even veiled in public.

In one of their more memorable discussions, they talked about domestic violence against women in the Muslim culture. Incredibly, Mack tried to explain why it was permissible in the Islamic culture for a man to physically discipline his wife. Stephanie listened incredulously to her tortured reasoning as to why this was acceptable. When Stephanie pointed out the historical record of the prophet Muhammad's violent history, as well as him having multiple wives, Mackenzie simply shrugged it off by saying he was granted special status and that made it okay.

> Incredibly, Mack tried to explain why it was permissible in the Islamic culture for a man to physically discipline his wife.

Sometimes, when Stephanie thought she'd made progress with Mackenzie, her hopes were dashed within a day or two. No matter what, we couldn't seem to change her mind about a religion that we knew she really didn't know or understand. When she couldn't explain or defend a position, her usual response was, "You can't understand because you're not Muslim." The sad reality was that

Mackenzie wasn't interested in finding answers. Stephanie likened it to pushing a string; you can make it change shape this way or that, but it never moves forward.

In retrospect, one of the first hints that something was up occurred one morning when Mackenzie came downstairs just in time to leave for class. She made a quick turn and plopped in a chair close to my desk. "Dad, I was thinking," she said. "When I go to Switzerland next year after I graduate, I think I may want to stay over there a little longer. You know, if I decide I want to go somewhere else, I want to be able to do it because I may never get to go there again. Maybe it would be better if I bought a one-way ticket."

Feeling a little annoyed, I looked up from my laptop. *Here we go again*, I thought, *she is always pushing the envelope*.

But there was no way Stephanie and I were going to go along with that. The brief discussion wasn't contentious, and for Mackenzie the request wasn't out of character. She had a tendency to try to push things further, so Stephanie and I took it in stride. After we told her we wouldn't agree to a one-way ticket, she didn't ask again. Months later, however, Stephanie and I would reflect back on that request.

As Mackenzie pulled further and further away from her faith and our family, our home was turning into something akin to reality TV. Not only were we having increasingly belligerent religious conflicts, Mackenzie was also pushing back on every rule we had in place. Simple chores like folding clothes turned into a battle, and she refused to clean up her room. Worse, her grades were falling dramatically at school. It seemed like every night included a conflict of some type. If it wasn't about religion, it was about her curfew, attitude, chores, grades, going to church, and on and on it went.

It was exhausting, but Stephanie and I remained true to the rules that governed our home. Not only was it important to us that we try to keep guardrails around Mackenzie, but we also had two younger boys who were watching the drama play out. We tried as best we could to shield them from the religious debates; therefore, most of the serious religious discussions took place after they went to bed.

The conflict in our home was weighing heavily on all of us, and our struggle with our daughter was getting much more difficult to keep to ourselves. Stephanie and I talked a lot, prayed a lot, and shed more than a few tears along the way. We vowed never to give up trying to figure out what was going on. We kept thinking there was some magic dust somewhere, that some person was going to have the right words, or the right person was going to cross paths with her and get her to wake up. We just didn't know when it was going to happen—or if it was going to happen at all.

CHAPTER 9

Burden Shared

John

As Mackenzie neared her eighteenth birthday in October 2013, Stephanie and I kept asking ourselves: *How did we get here?* Only five months earlier, everything was normal. We celebrated the end of the previous school year with Mack and her friends, by hosting a highly anticipated day at the lake. There was lots of food and drinks, and Mack and her friends spent several fun hours together wakeboarding and tubing.

Now, three months into her senior year of high school, those friends were nowhere to be found. With her eighteenth birthday approaching, Stephanie and I decided to do something Mack would love, in search of a breakthrough. We kept the surprise from Mack, and her birthday was a welcome reprieve from the constant stress and nightly arguments about religion and anything else that didn't suit her. For the first time in a long time, and if only for a single day, she seemed to be genuinely happy.

We opted for our traditional family celebration of Mack choosing her favorite restaurant (Joe's Crab Shack) for dinner, followed by cake and gifts at home. Mack, Luke, and Michael laughed and enjoyed being together for the first time in a long time. Our surprise gift was what we hoped would reignite some of her old passions and renew her friendships. Her face lit up when she opened the envelope and looked at the card, which read: "You Asked For It, You Got It!" We gave Mack a gift certificate for a tandem skydive, which was something she'd long said she wanted to do when she turned eighteen. The chances of us allowing our daughter to go up fourteen thousand feet and jump out of an airplane had been slim to none—until now. Stephanie and I were willing to try anything to bring her back. We invited Mack to bring all of her friends out to watch her jump, and then I'd grill steaks for them afterward at the airfield. She was thrilled! Finally, we saw the light and excitement return to our daughter's face. Perhaps this was the first step in getting her back.

Then, two weeks later, much to our dismay, Mackenzie changed her mind. She said the more she thought about it, the more she realized she didn't want to skydive, and asked if we could buy her a leather messenger bag instead. We were stunned at her request, but agreed to exchange the gift of adventure and camaraderie for a beautiful rich brown leather messenger bag. It was yet another tremendous blow to Stephanie and me.

By November, Mackenzie had become so withdrawn from the family that she was an island unto herself. Our friends and relatives were starting to notice that she was completely isolated, but nobody knew why. During the Thanksgiving holiday, we were visiting our parents and family in our hometown of Monroe, Louisiana, and one morning Mackenzie asked if she could go to Starbucks to study for an upcoming test. I dropped her off and returned three or four hours later to check on her.

As I approached her from behind, I noticed that she wasn't studying biology, but was intensely watching another Islamic video. I felt so disappointed and betrayed. I couldn't believe she would pass up spending time with her grandmother, aunts, uncles, and cousins—and us—to watch Islamic videos in a coffee shop.

In spite of everything we'd endured during the past three or four months, I kept thinking this would blow over. But when I saw her devoting hours to studying Islam during a family holiday, I realized that it was not going to simply run its course. I was genuinely afraid she was going to convert.

> As I approached her from behind, I noticed that she wasn't studying biology, but was intensely watching another Islamic video.

Stephanie and I have always leaned on each other through good times and bad. And together we have leaned on Christ to help us through the most difficult times. In the past, we had also leaned on family and friends when times got tough. We all need people we love and trust, even when we're embarrassed about what's going on in our lives. Stephanie and I were at the breaking point. We needed to open our circle of trust to get the help of others.

That night, I confided in my younger sister, Jill, about Mackenzie's sudden shift toward Islam. Jill was shocked and concerned, and we discussed it for a long time. There was no judgment from Jill, and I knew there wouldn't be. It felt good to share my concerns about Mack with her. Interestingly, that same night, unbeknownst to me, Stephanie shared the news with her sister, Debbie, as well. It was as if Stephanie and I had been hiding a terrible secret from our family and friends, and it was a relief that we weren't alone any longer.

In the coming days, I told my other sister, Kathy, and my mom about what was happening. Kathy hugged me, looked me in the eyes, and promised she would go anywhere at any time and do anything to help us. I told my brothers shortly afterward. I knew they would support Mackenzie and us, no matter what. Having a core family built on love, trust, and respect is my parents' greatest legacy—and we needed all the help we could get. Stephanie did the same thing for the same reasons, and it was reassuring to now have so many loved ones praying for us.

When Mackenzie found out that we'd told her grandmother, aunts, and uncles about what was going on, she was quite upset. We made no apologies. We explained to her that we were not going to keep something this important a secret from the people who cared for her and loved her deeply. If Mackenzie was, indeed, going to choose this road, she was going to have to do it in full view of her family.

After Thanksgiving, our religious discussions turned into Islamic attacks on Christianity. Nothing Stephanie or I said or did seemed to make a difference. In an act of pure desperation, I thought maybe there was a chance I could find someone from the Islamic community who would be willing to talk to Mack and tell her she needed to stay within her own faith. But who would it be, and how would I find him or her?

I thought about contacting Dr. George Mason, our former pastor at Wilshire Baptist Church in Dallas, who had long championed efforts in the region to build bridges between Christianity and other religions. It had been at least ten years since I'd talked to George, but I thought maybe it would be worth a shot. As I was driving back to Dallas, I called George's office and reached his assistant. I left George a message and asked him to call me back if he had time. Within minutes, George returned my call. I pulled off the highway and gave him a summarized version of Mackenzie's journey into Islam, including details of her obsessive studying and watching of Islamic videos. I asked George if he might know someone in the Islamic religion whom he trusted to talk to Mack and try to turn her away. Like I said, I was desperate. George said he didn't know anyone who he thought would be willing to do that, which was a disappointment, but not much of a surprise.

Then, for the next forty-five minutes, George advised me on kids in Mackenzie's age bracket, the formative nature of their minds, and how that impacts their judgment. He gave me practical advice on approaching difficult theological questions and how to address some of the other challenges we were facing. He even generously offered to talk to Mackenzie about any questions she had about Christianity, Islam, or any other topics.

Within days of our return home from Louisiana, the Islamic debates started once again. But this time, thanks to George's advice, I had a different tactic to tackle Mack's questions. First I suggested she talk to Pastor Sam, our longtime pastor at Parkway Hills Baptist Church. She quickly refused that offer, and I presumed it was because she had known Sam her whole life and didn't want to face him with this kind of discussion. I had anticipated her answer, so I then tossed out what I thought was a sure solution. I explained to Mackenzie that I had contacted Dr. Mason, and he had offered to talk to her one-on-one anytime she wanted. I reminded Mack that Dr. Mason was the pastor who had walked her down the aisle as an infant in that long-ago dedication ceremony, and I described his credentials to assure her that he would give her honest and reliable answers to her most difficult questions.

I watched Mackenzie intently as she considered my offer, but then she looked up and shook her head. She refused my offer and told me she wasn't interested in talking to George or Sam or anyone else. Stephanie and I realized we had just experienced another defining moment and our hearts sank because we realized that Mack had no interest in seeking answers. If Stephanie and I hadn't realized it before, we unequivocally knew it then: Mackenzie's mind was made up—she was going to convert to Islam and she wasn't turning back.

Mackenzie's mind was made up—she was going to convert to Islam and she wasn't turning back.

After that, Mackenzie's posture hardened and things quickly went from bad to worse. Our family was being torn apart at the seams. Night after night, Stephanie and I talked about what Mackenzie was doing, why she was doing it, and what we needed to do or say. We prayed for wisdom and that she would hold on to God. Everything we tried was unsuccessful.

Mackenzie

Aadam and I were talking regularly on the phone and via Skype. Our connection became closer, and we both struggled with the distance between us. Aadam still wanted to come to the United States to see me, and I wanted that too. He seemed to need me as much as I now needed him.

While I continued to fall for Aadam, everything else in my life seemed empty. I was cut off and isolated from everyone I'd trusted and cared for my entire life. I couldn't explain what I was feeling to my parents or anyone else. At times, I tried talking to my friends about Aadam and Islam, but they didn't understand. My friends were wrapped up in our senior year of high school, which was what I should have been doing, but at the time, I felt separated from everything happening around me at school.

By the time my senior year began, I wasn't hanging out with my friends at all. They would invite me to go swimming, but I no longer considered wearing a swimsuit appropriate. In fact, according to Aadam, my friends were considered "dirty" for having a boyfriend if they weren't planning on being together permanently. Once I started learning what a Muslim woman shouldn't do, which were things my friends did regularly, I began to look at my friends differently. They were doing things I'd done my entire life until I met Aadam, but that didn't matter anymore. I had grown so attached to him that I was only paying attention to what he told me.

In my mind, the only person who understood me was Aadam. I never imagined I would view the world so differently. When I talked to Aadam, he reminded me of the bigger picture. I became convinced that I was seeing the world for myself, instead of allowing my parents to point the way to a narrow, conservative view.

When I told Aadam about the tandem skydiving gift my parents gave me for my eighteenth birthday, he was extremely concerned. He told me that a good Muslim girl didn't put herself in dangerous situations like that. At first I was unsure what to do. I'd always wanted to go skydiving, and I was genuinely surprised my parents were allowing me to do it. In the end, however, my desire to please Aadam was so strong that I told my parents to exchange the gift certificate for a messenger bag. If my safety was that important to Aadam, I was willing to surrender something I'd been looking forward to for years. It wasn't the last time I would sacrifice something important in my life for him.

> My desire to please Aadam was so strong that I was willing to surrender something I'd been looking forward to for years.

My goals and thoughts were different now. My view of the world had shifted, and everything that was important in my life surrounded Aadam. I thought about him all the time and couldn't wait until I talked to him again. In retrospect, I should have seen how unhealthy our relationship was, how I had in a way become addicted to him. But I didn't realize my obsession at the time, and I only wanted to make him happy and plan for the time when we would be together.

Soon Thanksgiving was around the corner—a time I normally looked forward to for months, but this year I was dreading it. When we arrived at my relatives' homes in Louisiana, I tried my best to force a smile. I gave hugs to everyone and made small talk. It wasn't that I didn't want to be around them; it was actually quite the opposite. I longed for the closeness we had felt just the previous year. I felt isolated, and I knew my parents were hurting, but I couldn't let them see I was sad. I kept the same blank face I'd been showing for months.

On the day after Thanksgiving, I felt more and more like an outsider among my own family. No one said anything, but I knew they sensed something was wrong with me. I spent a lot of time sitting on the couch and texting Aadam, being careful not to let anyone see. Eventually I couldn't take it anymore, and I thought the only person I could feel comfortable with was Aadam, and I needed to see him. I asked my dad if I could go to Starbucks to get some homework done. He reluctantly took me, and I spent the next few hours talking with Aadam.

Once I was able to see Aadam's face, my sadness melted away. He treated me normal and told me that the only reason my family acted this way was because they didn't know what to say. As we talked, I felt myself regain confidence. I was no longer depressed and alone. He was like a drug. I felt anxious when I needed to see him but couldn't talk with him.

During that afternoon in Starbucks, the hours flew by while I chatted with Aadam, and then from the corner of my eye I saw my dad walking in the door behind me. I was overcome with sudden fear. I couldn't let him see Aadam! I quickly exited the Skype window on my computer. Of course, the next thing that popped up on my screen in its place was a YouTube video Aadam had shown me earlier about Islam. It filled my screen, and I didn't have time to close it before my dad approached me. He was visibly hurt and upset when he saw what he thought I'd been watching. He didn't say anything, as I packed my stuff and went to his car. The ride back to my relatives' house was silent. I stared out the window showing no emotion, but inside I felt alone and isolated.

I already longed for Aadam to comfort me again. But I also knew I had to keep him hidden from everyone else in my world.

CHAPTER 10

Deeper into His World

John

Christmas 2013 came and went in the Baldwin home without joy.

Like in most Christian homes, Christmas is usually the happiest of times. When we decorate the house, Stephanie puts on holiday music and everybody helps her set up a Christmas village, hang garlands on the bannister, and decorate our tree with eclectic ornaments, most of which carry some story as to who made it or where it came from. The prized decorations for Mackenzie, Luke, and Michael are ornaments Stephanie gave to them years ago. Each one reads "Mom's Favorite!"—and they all know it's true!

Mackenzie had always loved Christmas, especially when she was a little girl. On her first Christmas, Stephanie gave me a brightly decorated plate that read "Santa's Cookies." Every year when our kids were younger, I baked cookies with them, and we carefully set the plate out for Santa on Christmas Eve, just before they ran upstairs to wait for him. When Mackenzie was in the first grade, we gave her the biggest surprise she had ever received. After she saw the traditional unwrapped gifts from Santa, we told her to close her eyes and hold out her arms. Stephanie handed her a large wrapped box. When Mack tore the paper off, she found a bag of cat litter, a cat box, and a new collar. Tears started to form in her eyes, as she couldn't figure out why Santa would bring her all of those things and not a cat! Stephanie realized what was happening, and ran back to our bedroom to retrieve Molly, her first pet.

Many of our Christmas traditions have remained the same over the years. Every Christmas Eve, we attend church, sing traditional hymns, and listen to the Christmas message. The service at our church ends with us holding old-fashioned candles that are lit by touching your neighbor's lit candle. The worship center lights are then lowered, and the warm glow of the candles illuminates the walls as the congregation sings "Silent Night." On Christmas morning, Luke and Michael typically wake up long before Mackenzie and pile into her room until they're permitted to come downstairs. We make sure their gifts and a camera are in place before we call them down. It sounds like thunder as the kids scamper down the stairs. Once the gifts are opened, I serve my once-a-year Christmas breakfast of homemade cinnamon apple French toast and spicy sausage.

> Mackenzie asked if we were still planning to give her Christmas gifts, now that she no longer believed in Jesus.

Despite everything that was going on with Mackenzie, I hoped and wondered if Christmas might turn things around for us. Throughout the holidays, however, Mackenzie asked if we were still planning to give her gifts, now that she no longer believed in Jesus. She didn't sing Christmas carols that year. She tuned out the reading of the beautiful Christmas story given to us in Luke. On

Christmas Day, we gave Mackenzie her gifts like we always had, but the warm feeling of family togetherness was missing.

However, Stephanie and I thought we had another surefire idea. It was no secret that the ocean had been a constant source of fascination for Mack her entire life. Looking for anything to crack her thickening veneer, we decided to do something unexpected and irresistible for Christmas. We announced to the kids on Christmas morning that if everyone would agree to forgo their big birthday gifts in 2014, we would arrange for the entire family to get scuba-certified, and then take everyone diving while in Mexico for our goddaughter's wedding in July. Mackenzie had begged us for years to let her become scuba-certified. Her lifelong ambition to work with dolphins and orcas depended on her ability to dive, and she badly wanted to learn how to do it. We figured if anything would break her out of her self-constructed isolation, scuba diving was a guaranteed way to do it.

When we told Luke and Michael the plan, they exploded with excitement! But Mackenzie stunned us again with a pensive and quiet reaction. While the boys were literally still talking excitedly about the prospect of scuba diving in Mexico, Mackenzie simply said, "I'm not sure I want to do that." None of us could believe what we were hearing. She continued: "Yeah, that equipment is so heavy and stuff, and besides, I really want to free dive." The entire family was incredulous. "Are you kidding?" I asked her. "You've wanted to scuba dive your whole life!"

No matter how hard we tried, though, we couldn't say anything to change her mind. She didn't want to do it. Our family was in distress. We knew it, and felt powerless to change it. And we knew continuing down the same hopeless path was senseless.

In only six months' time, Mackenzie had traded her Christian heritage for Islam for no discernible reason. Separated almost totally from her circle of friends during her senior year, her grades were mediocre and her relationship with our family was slipping away.

No matter how hard Stephanie and I looked, we could not figure out what or who was behind it all. Her lack of friendships was perplexing. Mack had always loved being with friends; now she had gone weeks without seeing anyone. Even her longtime passion of working with marine mammals, which for years had been the subject of endless hours of reading, videos, and conversation, was barely mentioned.

The only thing Mack would discuss with us at any depth was her long-planned trip to Switzerland following her senior year, but even that had its share of oddities. For instance, we had given her travel books and maps for Christmas, hoping they would create some sort of neutral ground on which to talk to her.

But as the post-holiday weeks slipped by, the travel material remained untouched, where she had laid them on Christmas morning.

Mackenzie

Shortly after New Year's, Aadam asked me directly if I would visit a mosque. I wanted to make him happy, and I knew Islam was an important part of his life, but it was hard to envision me doing that. After weeks of inner turmoil, I knew I had to make a decision. I knew I was about to cross a threshold from which I might never return, and I struggled to find the determination to actually walk through the door.

One cold morning in February 2014, I found myself sitting in my car outside of a mosque not far from my home. It took me thirty minutes to muster the courage to go inside. I wasn't entirely sure why I was there; it felt so foreign to me. In my heart, I knew it was wrong. It felt wrong. But I believed I had to go in. I reached down, opened my car door, and stepped into the cold wind.

> I wasn't entirely sure why I was at the mosque, but I believed I had to go in. I reached down, opened my car door, and stepped into the cold wind.

I had planned to just walk into the mosque, but I knew there were rules I might not know and could accidentally break. Aadam warned me not to wear shoes inside and told me the rules were different at each mosque. I also realized that customs at mosques in Kosovo might be different from those in the United States. Entering such an unfamiliar place was incredibly intimidating. The mosque I visited was modern and massive; it covered what seemed to be three or four blocks. It had beautiful gray and tan stone, curved metal domes, and a lot of windows and doors.

As I built up the nerve to go into the mosque, I noticed a sign on a door that simply read "Men." There was another sign on the door written in Arabic. Obviously, I couldn't read Arabic, and I had no idea what the second sign meant. I didn't know what to do, so I stood there for a long time, trying to decide whether or not to go inside.

Unsure of what to do next, I began walking around the building when a couple approached me and asked if they could help. I told them I was interested in learning about Islam. The man introduced me to his wife, Samina, and she offered to give me a tour of the mosque. She was probably in her late twenties or early thirties. Samina told me she was Pakistani, and she was wearing a black robe and a colored scarf on her head. She was gentle and had a peaceful and caring presence. She was exceptionally respectful, especially toward her husband.

When we first walked into the mosque, the place smelled strange—like nothing I had experienced before, like some kind of chemical. It was definitely not incense. To be honest, I thought the smell was a result of worshippers not wearing shoes and having to use strong solutions to sanitize the floor. I noticed that most of the walls in the mosque were painted green. (Muslims associate green with paradise in the Koran, and it was supposedly the prophet Muhammad's favorite color.) There were tiled floors and tall ceilings. There were also worship rooms on the second floor, which were accessible by a back stairway. Given how beautiful the mosque looked from the outside, the stairwell was rather plain. It was built with painted metal stair treads, and the walls were covered in children's drawings. I couldn't help but notice the disparity between the appearance on the outside and inside of the mosque.

As we prepared to go upstairs to the worship area, they told me that people were praying, so we had to be quiet. Right before we went up the stairs, Samina pointed out where men prayed and informed me that women weren't permitted there. The women were separated from the men's worship area by glass, and the men were on the floor near the imam, or prayer leader, who was standing. Inside the worship hall, the floor had dark green carpet strips with gold lines outlining where to stand. Worshippers had their toes on the lines, with their feet together, as they prayed. We were standing above the worship area, tucked away in the back, and there was a loudspeaker on the ceiling so we could hear what was being said. Behind us was another room enclosed in glass, with the same carpet lines, for women with children. It was intended to block out the noise of the children.

During my first visit, I noticed there was clothing available for women to wear into the worship room. Per Islamic custom, Muslims wear modest, loose-fitting clothes to mosques. Muslim men often wear long pants, and women wear pants or full-length skirts or dresses, with long sleeves. Muslim women also typically wear a head scarf as well. This mosque had long, draping, dark green robes for women to wear, and they covered your hair and entire body. I didn't wear the garments on my first visit, but I eventually did.

Muslim women aren't supposed to reveal any skin, other than their faces and hands, in public. Dresses and pants are supposed to cover their ankles, and sleeves are supposed to reach their wrists. Women aren't supposed to wear clothes that are too clingy or tight either. The reason is they don't want men to be tempted by what they're wearing; you might compare it to the feeling of not wanting someone to see you in your underwear. Muslim women don't want anyone to see their figure, so only their husbands will know what they really look like.

After giving me a tour of the mosque, Samina told me she was excited to meet someone who was interested in Islam. We exchanged phone numbers, and she contacted me several days later, asking me to visit the mosque again. When she invited me to return, I instantly felt something in the pit of my stomach. I didn't want to go back, and I knew I shouldn't be there, but she was persistent and I didn't want to disappoint her. Throughout that week, I received many texts and phone calls from her, and at the end of the following week, I reluctantly agreed to return to the mosque.

I knew I was stepping deeper into Aadam's world.

CHAPTER 11

A Second Family

Mackenzie

The second time I went to the mosque was a little less awkward than the first, but it was still very difficult for me to go. To be honest, I really didn't want to go. I didn't want to return to a place where I was required to hide how uncomfortable I felt, but Aadam wanted me to go back. He wasn't being pushy about it, but I could tell he was really hoping I'd go. Besides, I had promised Samina that I would.

I wore different clothes the second time I went. I made sure I wore looser pants and a baggier, long-sleeved shirt. As I walked into the mosque, a woman named Tahani approached me. She told me she wanted to ask me a few questions about why I had decided to come and learn about Islam. I agreed to talk to her and followed her to a small room with desks. She asked me pretty basic questions about my family and why I was interested in Islam. I was honest and told her I'd become very involved with a Muslim man. Tahani and I had been talking for about ten minutes when we were suddenly interrupted by a man singing in Arabic over the loudspeaker. It caught me by surprise. Tahani apparently noticed I was confused, and she smiled and told me it was the azan.

"Isn't it just beautiful?" she asked me.

I had never heard the sound before. I had no idea what the man was saying, but I have to admit it was incredible. It sounded as if he was pouring his heart out while singing the song. "This is sung about five minutes before every time we pray," Tahani explained. "It lets everyone know they should come to pray. Come on!"

She jumped out of her chair and grabbed my hand. She guided me up the stairs and took me into the worship room with the other women. I had never felt more out of place in my entire life. "Just do what I do," Tahani whispered to me.

I had never even attempted to recite an Islamic prayer before, and I had no idea what to expect. I looked around as the imam recited a few sentences in Arabic. My hands were folded in front of me, mimicking the women standing around me. I carefully made sure my feet were in the right place as well. All of a sudden, everyone bowed. I copied them. In the middle of the prayer, we dropped to our knees and stood up again. I couldn't help but look around and study what everyone else was doing.

> It felt good for someone to hug me and be so happy about something I did. I hadn't felt that way in months.

When the prayer was over, Tahani gave me a huge hug and congratulated me. Although I wasn't overly ecstatic about the prayer, I have to admit it felt good for someone to hug me and be so happy about something I did. I hadn't felt that way in months, and I couldn't help but smile. Tahani and I continued to talk until I decided to head home. On the drive back to my house, I kept thinking about what had just occurred. I had mixed emotions about it. When I talked to Aadam that night, I told him that I had prayed with the Muslim women, and he was overjoyed. He couldn't stop asking me questions about what I'd experienced and felt at the mosque. I had never seen him so happy for me.

The Islamic prayers at the mosque were always recited in Arabic, so I didn't really know their meanings. I basically memorized the first forty-five seconds of a prayer, and that's really about all I understood. The way Muslims pray is very ritualistic: they fold their arms, fall to their knees, and rise up and down. I eventually learned how many times to do these things, but I felt no freedom while I was praying. It didn't seem natural to me. Muslims are required to pray five times a day, but I honestly didn't worry too much if I missed a prayer. The mosque was never overly crowded, and I skipped prayers if I thought there was going to be a lot of people there.

As I became more involved at the mosque, I learned many of the Islamic customs. I learned that you must wash your body before you pray. This includes washing your hands three times, as well as your face, arms, and feet. The washing occurred at a regular sink. Muslims are required to remove their shoes before they walk into the prayer room because they don't want the carpet or floors on which they pray to be dirty. It's customary to enter the mosque with the right foot first and exit with the left foot first (I'm not exactly sure why). The typical Arabic greeting is "Asalaam Alaykum," which means "Peace be upon you," and the proper response to a greeting is "Wa Alaykum Asalaam," which means "And peace be upon you also."

Once I committed to worshipping at the mosque, things started moving really fast with Aadam. The women I met there advised me that I shouldn't be talking to Aadam unless we were engaged. Of course, the simple solution for me was to simply tell them that we were, indeed, getting married. I figured it might actually be a possibility one day, but I mostly said it to get the people at the mosque off my back. But once I told them that Aadam and I were engaged and I was going to meet him in Switzerland, they were willing to do anything to help us.

With Aadam's encouragement, I started going to the mosque several times a week to pray, even though I felt uncomfortable when I was there. I started spending more and more time at the mosque once I met Tahani. She invited me to many events and prayer times to get to know other people who worshipped there. I wasn't hanging around with my high school friends anymore. In fact, I really didn't have any friends.

It was quite a drastic change for me because I was very social growing up, and I was typically with at least two friends at any given time. I missed being with my friends, but I learned from Aadam that they weren't living their life in a good way. They were doing things that were not in line with my newly kindled beliefs. Don't get me wrong: I felt guilty leaving them, especially my best friend. We had been through so much, and I felt as if I had abandoned her, but I couldn't think about it. I had to keep moving forward with what I was starting to realize was the right path, the path that led to God and, more importantly, the path that led to Aadam.

After I'd prayed with Tahani a few more times, she introduced me to some teenage girls who attended the mosque. They talked to me in depth about my journey to Islam and seemed genuinely concerned about how I was doing. They told me that I inspired them to stay on the right path and to help other young Muslims. I enjoyed their company. I hadn't had a real conversation with someone my age in more than a month. I didn't feel so isolated and alone anymore. I exchanged phone numbers with a few of them, and we exchanged text messages over the next couple of weeks.

A Second Family

During one of my visits to the mosque, Tahani told me she wanted to talk to me about something important. I'd told her that I'd been constantly fighting with my parents about Islam. In fact, I'd told her that I felt like I didn't have much of a family anymore. She introduced me to a woman named Hadiya and her daughter, Amira. When I met them for the first time, I smiled and introduced myself. Tahani told me that Hadiya and Amira would act as my second family if I wanted. She told me they would be there for me for anything I needed and would welcome me into their home with open arms. I wasn't sure how to react to the offer. I thanked them for being so generous and for their willingness to spend time with me.

Hadiya invited me to dinner at their house the next night. I decided I wanted to go. Why not? I have to admit I was pretty nervous as I approached their house the next day. I didn't know them, and

> She told me that Hadiya and Amira would act as my second family if I wanted. They would welcome me into their home with open arms.

I had no idea what to expect. I knocked on the door and waited. When the door opened, I saw Hadiya standing there with a giant smile on her face. I instantly smiled back at her. It was such a welcome sight. She was a larger woman with a loud, booming voice and a huge personality. She was wearing an olive-colored shirt and soft flowy pants. She must have seen my surprise that she wasn't wearing a hijab (head scarf). She explained, "We are family here. We don't have to wear the scarfs with each other."

As I walked into their house, I was quiet and they could tell I was nervous. Hadiya invited me into the kitchen to help her cook. I had never eaten Pakistani food before; it smelled of strong, sweet spices that I was unfamiliar with. I helped her chop vegetables and set the table. As I ate dinner with them, I quickly became incredibly comfortable. I asked them many questions about Islam and what it's like to live a Muslim life. Hadiya patiently answered my questions and gave me so much confidence. I told her about the problems I was having with my parents at home, and I could tell she hurt for me. She took my hands and looked into my eyes. She told me my parents' reaction was normal, and I couldn't blame them for being upset. She assured me that they loved me and everything would be okay with time. I could feel tears filling my eyes. I hadn't felt that much compassion in so long.

Over the next several weeks, I became much more comfortable with Hadiya and Amira. Once I became close to them, I started going to the mosque more frequently and actually began looking forward to it. Hadiya even started calling me her "other daughter." She proved to be one of the most compassionate women I had ever known. Amira was a year younger than me and was incredibly respectful and responsible. Hadiya eventually told me that they would be a family for me when I felt like I didn't have one. And on multiple occasions, when I was fighting with my parents and felt broken, I'd call Hadiya and ask if I could come see them. She would invite me to her home, and I'd spend the late afternoon laughing and eating dinner with my "new family."

I never wore a hijab in public, but I had to wear one in order to pray. I was using one the mosque provided, and honestly it was quite ugly. It was dark green and very long. It fit over my head and went to the floor to hide my figure. I didn't like wearing it, but it was required of women in the mosque. One day, Hadiya asked me to come to her car because she wanted to show me something. She opened the trunk and there was a box full of hijabs and outfits to wear at the mosque. She said they were Amira's, but she had outgrown them. They were beautiful, and I felt overwhelmed by her generosity.

I thanked Hadiya and gave her a long hug. After that moment of kindness, Hadiya and Amira were like my second family. In fact, I spent more time with them than with my real family. I trusted them and they loved me. For the first time in a while, I felt like I was no longer alone.

My parents didn't know anything about me worshipping at the mosque. I kept it a secret from them at all times and from my friends for several weeks. My mom and dad knew about my growing interest in Islam, but they still didn't know about Aadam. Aadam had me convinced that Islam was the true religion, and that the Koran proved something the Bible didn't. My dad always seemed to have answers to my doubts about Christianity, but I didn't want to hear them. I wanted to believe that Islam was good because if it wasn't right, then I couldn't be with Aadam.

> I wanted to believe that Islam was good because if it wasn't right, then I couldn't be with Aadam.

I was no longer myself. I was drifting further away from my parents, and I knew I was hurting them. When I voiced concerns about alienating my family to Aadam, he told me that they were Christians and were confused. One day my dad said to me, "I would give anything to have things go back to normal."

So would I, but I'm in too deep, I thought to myself.

In my mind, my real family was rejecting me—and what I had become. Sadly, I didn't realize then that I was the one rejecting them.

CHAPTER 12

Love Her Where She's At

John

The final straw for me came in February when I heard unusual sounds behind the closed door of Mackenzie's bedroom. Without knocking, I opened the door and saw her kneeling in a Muslim prayer position on a quilt my mother had made. I was shocked and outraged by what I saw. "Are you crazy?" I asked her. "What are you doing? That's my mother's quilt! This is a Christian home!"

It was time for us to take a much stricter stance. We pulled Mackenzie aside and told her we would not allow our family to fall apart because of the chaos and heartache she was causing. We explained to her that while we couldn't control what she believed, we could control what happened in our home.

We said we were not going to risk our boys being confused about which religion they needed to be following, and at that point she was beginning to confuse them. Therefore, we told Mack that she was not allowed to talk to her younger brothers about religion, and her Islamic materials had to be removed from our house, including her Koran, Islamic books, and commentaries. We also told her that Islamic videos and music were not to be played in our house, including in her room, any longer.

As I reflected on what was happening to my family, it was evident that even though I understood my responsibilities as a father, they were at a near-total loss:

- *Raise your kids so they don't want to disappoint you.* Clearly this was the last thing on Mackenzie's mind.
- *Raise your children under the Word of God and they won't stray from it.* She was outright rejecting it.
- *Raise your kids so they know you love them and they will love you back.* That was slipping away from us fast.

Mackenzie's heart and mind had changed radically, and after months of trying to find a breakthrough, I broke down. Stress, despair, dread, and outright shock flooded my soul. As I stood in our living room trying to compose myself, I looked up and saw Mackenzie coldly unloading the dishwasher. She was stone-faced, unfazed, and unmoved by the spectacle. I knew then that my daughter was gone, and I knew I had failed as a father.

> I knew then that my daughter was gone, and I knew I had failed as a father.

Out of ideas and desperate to figure out what was happening, I told Stephanie it was time for us to take a step back to assess what to do next. First, we knew that everything we had tried up to this point wasn't working. Second, we knew something different needed to be done—and we had to do it now.

We decided to see a family counselor for a different perspective. We knew Mackenzie would not willingly participate in counseling, and we didn't ask her to go. We knew it wouldn't be a magic bullet to make our problems go away. But we definitely needed an outside perspective as to what was going on. In short, we needed someone to help us see the forest and not the trees, so we set an appointment.

I'll be honest: My attitude in these counseling sessions swung from reflective to flat-out anger, especially when the conversation turned to her Islamic conversion. When the subject of Islam came up, I'd feel myself tense as the anger and frustration mounted inside. My body language shifted and the tone of my voice changed instantly. It made me so mad she would do this!

Then a remarkable thing happened. The counselor called me on it. She had been observing me over the hours we had been together and asked why it made me so angry. I know I must have looked at her like she was some kind of a nut. *Are you serious? Why am I angry?* I explained to the therapist that I had tried my best to teach Mackenzie the value of her Christian heritage. I had shared Scripture and my own faith with her through example and times of hardship. We had prayed with our kids regularly. I was a deacon in the church, for goodness' sakes! Our families were devout Christians for generations! I had a duty as a father to ensure that Mackenzie was raised in the Christian faith, and now she was simply dumping all of it for no apparent reason. And she was trading it in for Islam, of all things! *And you're asking me why I'm angry?*

Then I stopped talking. Stephanie was at my side the entire time and interjected nothing. The counselor paused a few seconds before responding. Looking directly at me, she said quietly, but firmly, "John, it's not about *you*." I stared at her blankly as those words soaked in. She continued, "Like it or not, she has the right to live her own life, to believe what she wants to believe, and become what she wants to become. She may grow up to be a circus clown, but that is her choice. As a parent, you may not like it or agree with it, but it is her decision to make. You did everything you were supposed to do and did the best you could. She will either accept it or reject it. Either way, it is her life to live and her choice to make."

> "Like it or not, she has the right to live her own life, to believe what she wants to believe, and become what she wants to become."

Okay, I'll admit that stung a bit, but I had to admit she was right. I was angry in large part because Mackenzie's choices were a reflection on me as a father, Stephanie and me as parents, and our family's reputation. I will admit that I was thoroughly embarrassed by what was happening in my home. To think that I might one day have to tell someone that my daughter had left Christianity and was now Muslim was so far out of my range of possibilities that I could not imagine saying it. In fact, I never told anyone outside of my family and pastors. I was too embarrassed to explain what was going on and why we couldn't stop it.

I finally replied back to the counselor, "You know, you're right." I was going to have to come to grips with the fact that there was a very real possibility that she might convert to Islam. I was going to have to rely on God and trust He would guide her home. And I was going to have to quit worrying about how this reflected on me, and open up to our family and friends about it. Mackenzie was eighteen years old, a legal adult, and we were going to have to accept this may not turn out the way we wanted.

Coincidentally, during this same window of time I received another piece of advice that helped me frame a new approach. Our church sponsored a men's breakfast featuring a local speaker named "Smokey John" Reaves. Smokey John owns a barbecue joint near

Love Field Airport in Dallas and had been giving unvarnished spiritual advice to men in the Dallas/Fort Worth area for many years. According to Smokey John's testimony, he abused alcohol and rejected God when he was younger. But then a man approached him at his restaurant and asked if he could talk with him about Christianity. For some reason, Smokey John agreed to meet with him.

On the morning of the appointment, the man went to Smokey John's house at seven o'clock as scheduled, and Smokey John was sleeping off a long night of drinking. Obviously, he was in no mood or condition to talk about Christianity with anyone. But with some rather forceful help from his wife, Gloria, Smokey John climbed out of bed, threw on some clothes, and walked out to meet the stranger who had come to befriend him. Smokey John said that morning changed his life. After a couple of additional morning meetings, Smokey John finally asked his friend why he was so worried about his salvation. Why did he keep coming to see him when he had disrespected him so much at their initial meeting? Why did the man still care after Smokey John had repaid his kindness by showing up smelly, half drunk, half dressed, and with a bad attitude?

At this point, I was very much absorbed in my own problems, but now I took notice and listened closely as Smokey John finished his story. *"I'm just going to love you where you're at,"* Smokey John recalled the man saying. And with that simple statement, God had delivered the message I needed to hear. I needed to love Mackenzie where she was, regardless of where it was. I couldn't understand what she was doing or why she was doing it, but it wasn't about me. I went home and told Stephanie that from then on, I was going to love Mackenzie where she was, no matter where that was. I was going to love her unconditionally: Muslim or Christian, circus clown or animal trainer. And it changed everything for me. It gave me something to center on and a place to come back to, especially when I was on the brink of giving up on her.

The next week, our family counselor advised us that Mackenzie's actions were most likely a huge display of independence and rebellion, and that we should quit pushing her so hard. If we let it go, the counselor believed it would go away in a couple of months. We agreed to give Mackenzie some space. Certainly, actively opposing her conversion to Islam from a theological and cultural standpoint hadn't worked, so we figured we might as well try something different.

From that night forward, Stephanie and I didn't make a big display when we debated Islam with Mackenzie. We quit "taking the bait," even though Mack continued to bring it up often. As we turned a deaf ear to her arguments about Christianity, the frequency of the discussions and the tone of them decreased dramatically. Make no mistake: We were no less distraught about Mackenzie's conversion, but what the counselor told us made sense. Mackenzie had always pushed back on boundaries, and we hoped that was the case now. Stephanie and I spent less time fighting Mackenzie about religion, and we kept praying that Christ would intercede to bring her home.

But we knew it was not the end of our troubles. Mackenzie was aggressively pulling away from family and friends, and we were ready to do whatever we could to break the cycle. In our hearts, Stephanie and I clung to Proverbs 22:6, which tells us, "Start children off the way they should go, and even when they are old they will not turn from it." Our prayer became, "Someday she'll circle back." Christianity was planted in Mackenzie from the time she was six weeks old. We knew the Truth was in her heart and that at one point in time she had believed it. We knew her faith might have been covered up, but we prayed it would flourish again someday.

If nothing else, our new, less aggressive approach with Mack immediately settled down the religious strife at home, which was a welcome relief not only to us, but also for Luke and Michael. As hard as we tried to shield them from it, they had been experiencing the escalating tension for months. We also had extra company with us at this time, as Stephanie's parents had moved into our home full-time. Her father was in very bad health and was facing a series of back surgeries. Stephanie and I were more than happy to help them through a difficult time, of course, but having them there changed the dynamic of our house substantially. That's one of the reasons it was so important to come to some sort of a truce with Mackenzie.

In the meantime, with an absence of friends, Mackenzie threw herself wholly into an unquenchable desire to save as much money as possible for her planned trip to Switzerland, working nearly thirty hours a week at a fast-food restaurant. Stephanie and I repeatedly tried to get her to reconnect with her group of friends, but she wasn't interested in having any sort of social life. Besides, her friends were now "immature" or "didn't share the same interests anymore." Months had gone by without Mack having a date or having friends come over to our house like in the past. She spent all of her free time working.

One of the more difficult moments for me, personally, was when Mackenzie declined to attend the highly anticipated High Adventure Treks Sweetheart Banquet in February. It is a tradition in which graduating senior girls reunite with old friends, laugh about the adventures they shared together from fifth to tenth grade, review their accomplishments, and announce college plans to the HATS community. It is a special night.

Mackenzie and I had attended these banquets every year since she was in the sixth grade. But during the year in which Mack was supposed to be honored, she told me she couldn't get off work. I knew better, but I chose not to confront her about it. I attended the banquet anyway, helping with the preparations and behind-the-scenes work required for the evening. Seeing the other senior girls enjoying a final HATS evening with their dads while my daughter chose to work instead of attending with me was very painful.

Seeing the other senior girls enjoying a final HATS evening with their dads while my daughter chose to work instead of attending with me was very painful.

I kept reminding myself throughout the evening that I needed to love her where she was at, but it really hurt.

CHAPTER 13

Change of Plans

Mackenzie

By March 2014, I was becoming more and more excited about traveling to Switzerland. Aadam and I had so many plans, and I even had maps and itineraries for our activities. We had each day planned out for what we were going to do. We would daydream for hours about the trip, and every time we talked about it, we came up with a new idea of something to do.

Aadam's family barely made ends meet, so this trip was especially exciting for him because he'd never done anything like it before. We planned to do a lot of hiking in the mountains since we both loved the outdoors. We also planned to visit Lake Geneva. As the day drew closer, I could only imagine how exciting it would be to finally be with Aadam in a new and beautiful country. I was planning to stay in Zurich, so there would be plenty to do right there as well. It was going to be such a phenomenal trip.

One day after school, Aadam and I were in a Skype session,

but something was wrong. Aadam had that same distant attitude he'd had a few months earlier, when he told me he couldn't travel to New York. He didn't talk much and seemed very upset. When I asked what was wrong, he told me the worst news I could imagine: he couldn't make it to Switzerland. He could sense I was very upset, and started crying, which instantly made me lower my tone and calm down. He said it was too expensive to fly, and he couldn't even afford a train ticket.

> When I asked what was wrong, he told me the worst news I could imagine.

I felt totally defeated, and in my heart I knew there was no way we'd see each other. Now all the time we'd spent talking to each other for the last eleven months felt worthless. I thought about everything we'd been through together—the times I needed someone when I felt like I didn't have a family, the hours I'd spent talking to him on the phone or Skype.

When I was at my lowest point in that conversation, Aadam told me there was one more option: I could travel to Kosovo and meet him. Instantly I felt a gnawing in my stomach. I didn't want to go there. I'd seen news stories about girls leaving their country to go be with a man, and who never returned. I told him I didn't think it was a good idea. He seemed a little hurt that I dismissed the idea so quickly.

"Do you not trust me?" he asked.

I looked down, trying not to choke on my words.

"I—I do trust you," I said. "I'm just not sure it's a good idea."

Aadam could tell I was having a hard time answering him.

"Just think about it," he said.

We said good night and I sat on my bed, feeling deflated. It was an all-too-familiar feeling—the same disappointment I'd felt when he backed out of meeting me first in New York, and then again in Switzerland. The next few days we continued to talk, but there wasn't much excitement in our conversations. In fact, it was a bit depressing. We could no longer talk about any of the fun things we planned to do or see. I still longed to see him, and even though we had never been physically together, I missed him.

I grabbed my computer and typed in "Kosovo." Photographs of neighborhoods with tiny houses crammed together came up on my screen. It didn't look very appealing to me, to be honest. When I told Aadam that I was exploring Kosovo on the Internet, he sent me a link. When I clicked on the link, I was taken to a pinned location on Google Maps. I zoomed in and saw a small house located next to green hills. Aadam told me it was where he lived. He said he knew I was worried about going to Kosovo, but if I saw where he lived, maybe I would change my mind. I have to admit, it looked pretty nice. It wasn't secluded, but it wasn't right next to another house either.

Aadam told me that although the city where he lived wasn't as nice as Zurich, it was still decently large and he would love to show me his country. I still felt uneasy. It was one thing to meet him somewhere neutral, and another to meet him in his own hometown.

It took me several weeks, but after a lot of research and soul-searching, I finally decided I would go to Kosovo. I was still unsure about what I was doing, and that feeling never went away, but I trusted Aadam. I wanted to see him—I had to see him. At that point, he was the only one who understood me—in a deep way, even more than Hadiya and Amira. I felt like going to Kosovo was my only option.

Without Aadam, I wasn't happy, and the idea of never being able to see him was unbearable to me. I told Aadam I would come to Kosovo. When I told him I was coming, he told me he lived near a United States Army base and could call the U.S. Embassy to inform them that I was there. The plan doesn't make sense to me now, but at the time I was only trying to connect the dots of what I was committing myself to. I accepted what he said as an honest expression of goodwill. A few nights later, he sent me a video made with the iPhone I'd sent him. It was a video of Aadam and his friends sitting at a café. His friends told me how excited they were to meet me. I felt more at ease knowing there were so many people looking forward to meeting me.

I started planning my trip to Kosovo, but I obviously wouldn't be telling my parents.

With so many doors closing around Aadam and me, I knew that I'd have to go to him if we were going to be together. I'd taken a job at a local fast-food restaurant with the intention of earning as much money as possible. I'd saved $6,000. My first plan was to use the money to pay for airline tickets for Aadam to fly to New York, and me to travel to meet him there. Then I planned to use it for our time in Switzerland. And now it seemed that the only way I would ever see him was if I went to Kosovo.

I was a little scared about traveling to an unfamiliar place to meet a man I'd never met in person. Although Aadam had spent so much time talking with me and trying to convert me to Islam, I felt like he truly cared about me. He had spent a year building a relationship with me, and I didn't see any reason to be afraid of him. I believed in my heart that he truly wanted to be with me, and I definitely wanted to be with him.

Of course, I never wanted to leave the United States or my family. Even though my parents didn't understand what I was doing or why I was doing it, I still loved them. I loved my little brothers and didn't want to leave them behind. It wasn't in my wildest dreams that I'd ever have to abandon my family, but after a while it became clear that I would have to go to Kosovo if I was going to be with Aadam. Things were getting complicated, and I was feeling uncomfortable about the situation, but I was in too deep and felt it was too late to simply back out.

At this point, Aadam was also becoming extremely controlling with me, which should have been another red flag. I was getting annoyed by his behavior, but I'd been going to the mosque regularly for a couple of months and witnessed how men and women interacted there, so I believed his controlling behavior was acceptable in the Muslim culture. Whenever I did something Aadam didn't approve of, he would scold me and tell me that it looked bad when a Muslim woman did that. Then he would correct me and instruct me on how I should behave. He would often tell me that I shouldn't be staying out late at work because it was too dangerous for a girl. Since he told me that women in Kosovo

> Whenever I did something Aadam didn't approve of, he would scold me and tell me that it looked bad when a Muslim woman did that.

rarely stayed out after dark because of crime, I justified his behavior as only being concern for me. After all, he didn't know how safe it was where I lived. Much like when he discouraged me from going skydiving on my eighteenth birthday, Aadam would often tell me what I should and shouldn't do based on my safety. In a lot of ways, I considered him to be my protector, who only had my best interests at heart. So his concern for me made sense in a way, at least at the time.

As the end of my senior year of high school approached, my relationship with Aadam became more intense. I was still torn on what I should do; 75 percent of me wanted to go to Kosovo, and 25 percent of me wanted to stay.

It's hard to explain why I was so attracted and so attached to Aadam. I felt closer to him and his family than to my own. I never had a real conversation with Aadam's parents because he told me they couldn't speak much English. From what I saw of them during our video chats, they seemed like very nice people. During a few of my Skype sessions with Aadam, his father stopped behind him and made funny faces at me that Aadam couldn't see. His dad waved and smiled at me a lot. One time, his parents sat down in front of the computer together, and Aadam told me that he would translate for us. I talked to his parents for a few minutes, and they told me they were extremely excited that Aadam met me, and they couldn't wait until I came there to meet them.

Aadam's family always expressed how excited they were that I was coming to Kosovo. In the Muslim religion, it's common for young people to be engaged without having met the other person. In fact, it was so acceptable to them that it was easy for me to feel normal about what I was doing.

At that point, I felt decently safe with Aadam and his family. One time I joked with Aadam that I could help his mother in the kitchen and lend a hand on the farm, because I didn't think I'd be able to get a job in Kosovo. Aadam told me that he would rather I be at home anyway, because women in his culture tended to take care of the children and do household chores. I'd never imagined being a housewife, but the idea eventually grew on me. I decided that I could be happy doing it, as long as I was with Aadam.

John

As spring neared, Stephanie and I encouraged Mackenzie to finalize her plans about going to Switzerland. If Mackenzie was going to go, she needed to put her plans in motion, and we also felt the trip would be something that we could connect with her about. The trip had been discussed in general terms for several months, but she had yet to set a date, purchase an airline ticket, or form an agenda of activities. Once she found a date that would mutually work for our family friends in Switzerland and us, we would reach out to them to thank them for hosting her and inform them about our parameters for her stay.

Even though Mack was relentlessly saving for the trip, she had done almost nothing in terms of logistics or preparation. Her inaction about something that important wasn't unprecedented; Mack was above all else a procrastinator, but this was unusual even for her, given her apparent excitement about the trip. We noticed she wasn't doing a lot of research or making any kind of reservations at all. It was baffling to us, but when we asked her about the trip, she would tell us that she was talking to her friend Miriam—the friend she was supposed to meet in Switzerland—and they were working out the details.

As part of our graduation present, we planned to arrange a nice excursion that we knew she couldn't afford, something really memorable. But without a specific time frame for her travel, we couldn't make the arrangements. Despite her lack of planning, she continued focusing on saving money for the trip.

That spring there were two Plano West Senior High School events that traditionally occur in the final weeks of a student's senior year. A really special event happens when the seniors return to their elementary schools to see each other, rekindle old grade-school friendships, and visit with their favorite teachers. It is truly a special day that is well known and highly attended each year. For whatever reason, Mackenzie flatly refused to go. She provided no real reason to us, and none of our cajoling or encouragement made a difference. The morning of the event, she slept in and let it pass, evidently without a thought.

The other special event was, of course, the Plano West High School junior-senior prom. Mackenzie had never had a shortage of invitations to dances, but as prom night approached we heard nothing from her about a date, plans for a new dress, or anything related to it. Finally, Stephanie asked her about the prom, and Mackenzie said she wasn't really interested in going. She told Stephanie she believed the kids were too immature for her now and she really didn't want to attend. Several different guys invited her to the prom, but she turned down every one. Nothing we said would dissuade her. She worked until midnight on the night of her senior prom.

We hated to see Mack miss her senior prom and everything else important in what should have been one of the most memorable years of her life. Instead, she traded those memories for arguments about religion and late nights working at a fast-food restaurant. But it was the path she chose, even as we tried to change her mind. While Mackenzie occasionally spoke about anticipating graduation and even briefly mentioned starting college, she rarely wanted to discuss her future with us. The time we spent together was at an all-time low. She spent little time at home, no time with her friends, and many hours at work.

While the outright signs of her Islamic interests and potential conversion were suppressed, we knew they had not disappeared. Every Sunday morning was a battle over whether or not she was going to join us for church. But as long as she was living in our home, we told her, she was going to go. It was a constant struggle.

On the morning of May 12, I left for a four-day business trip to Wilmington, Delaware. As I left our house that Monday morning, I couldn't have known that it would be a business trip I'd never forget.

CHAPTER 14

Lightning Strikes

John

On the morning of Tuesday, May 13, 2014, I was huddled around a conference table at the technological headquarters of one of the world's largest banks, trying to figure out a difficult mathematics model. As my colleague Cindy and I listened intently to a data analyst on a conference call, my cell phone buzzed with a text message.

I glanced at my phone and noticed it was a text message from Scot, one of our close friends from High Adventure Treks. I wasn't sure that he had ever contacted me outside of a HATS question. "John, this is Scot. Please call me right away," the message read.

I feared something might be terribly wrong, so I broke away from the meeting and moved to an adjacent conference room to dial Scot's cell number. He immediately answered and thanked me for calling him back so quickly.

"What's up?" I asked.

Scot is a highly polished professional, but that morning he was clearly struggling to find the right words. After a few starts and stops, he finally said, "There's no good way to say this, John. I'm really sorry, but has Mackenzie ever said anything to you about Islam?"

I was shocked. *How in the world does he know about that?* I wondered.

Once I gathered my thoughts, I confirmed to Scot that, indeed, Mackenzie was exploring Islam and we'd been dealing with it for a while.

"Why?" I asked him.

Scot once again paused, and I could tell he was still searching for a way to tell me what he knew. Finally, he said, "I don't know how else to share this other than just to tell you straight up. John, I'm sorry to tell you this: Mackenzie is planning to leave the country and marry a Muslim guy she has met online. I think he's in Albania. She's planning to leave the country in the next two weeks and has instructed anyone who knows not to tell you until she gets there."

> "Mackenzie is planning to leave the country and marry a Muslim guy she has met online."

I was stunned.

"What? I'm sorry. What did you say?"

Scot repeated it.

"Mackenzie is planning to marry a Muslim guy she met online. She's planning to leave the country without telling you guys. She's planning to leave in two weeks. I'm sorry to tell you this, John, but we felt like you had to know."

As my mind raced in a million directions, I listened silently as Scot explained what he knew. Mackenzie had been telling his daughter, Sarah, and their mutual friend, Jordyn, about a guy she met on a social media site. Mackenzie and this guy had been talking about religion for several months, and recently she told the girls that she had converted to Islam and was going to catch a plane to marry him. The girls had been trying to talk her out of it, but she was insistent.

"She told the girls that if you guys find out, she'll leave the next day," Scot told me.

I asked a few more questions, but I honestly don't remember what they were. I do remember Scot finishing our conversation with something like, "I don't know much more. Jeff has more details, and you really need to call him. I don't have any idea what to tell you to do. John, I'm so sorry. I can't imagine how this feels. You know we love both of you. I'm sorry to bring you news like this, but you had to know what was going on."

I sincerely thanked Scot for calling me and told him I knew how hard this had to be for him to tell me. Then I hung up. I knew it was true. I didn't doubt it for a minute. Mackenzie's behavior over the last year had changed so quickly and so dramatically, and now pieces in what was a bizarre puzzle were finally falling into place.

Standing in that empty, dark conference room in Wilmington, Delaware, the reality of what I had just heard began to sink in. I felt numbing shock. Not anger—that would come later. The sound I heard in my head was like a gun going off too close to you without ear protection. It was a huge bang, then ringing. It felt exactly like that.

I tried to collect myself and then returned to my meeting, where Cindy was still working intently with the bank's technical team on their problems. I sat down and tried to refocus on the task at hand, but it was impossible. She glanced over at me and then, evidently concerned with my demeanor, muted the phone and asked if everything was okay. I looked at her blankly and said, "I just got some terrible news about my daughter. I've got to go outside for a few minutes." I got up from the table and walked out.

I left the building and made my way to a small park the bank maintains for its employees. I found a table and sat for several long minutes in silent disbelief, trying to absorb what I had just heard. As the fog in my mind slowly cleared, more revelations began to hit me.

She was going to leave without even telling us? Without even saying good-bye to her brothers? How could she do that to us? She is marrying someone she met online? What is she thinking?

The unanswered questions and shock from what I had heard flooded my brain. I was overwhelmed, trying to comprehend what was happening, and I felt tears streaming down my face. Then the shock was replaced by anger and fear. The plethora of uncontrollable emotions came in waves. Finally, I prayed. I prayed for help, and that's all I remember asking God for. After forty-five minutes or so, I finally collected myself and remembered that Scot said our friend Jeff had more details. I decided to call him and find out what he knew.

Jeff and his daughter, Jordyn, are also our good friends from HATS. Mackenzie, Jordyn, and Sarah had become particularly close, especially since the ninth grade. Jeff was expecting my call and picked up immediately. He began providing more details about what was happening. Jeff told me that Sarah and Jordyn had advised them that Mackenzie had been talking about this plan for a few weeks. Jeff said he was sorry that the girls hadn't told them sooner, but they kept thinking it would blow over. But now their girls were convinced Mack was serious, and they were very afraid for her. Sarah and Jordyn said they would never be able to forgive themselves if something happened to her. He and Scot knew I needed to know right away.

I listened as Jeff talked and didn't say anything as he continued. He knew Mackenzie was interested in Islam, but hadn't realized it was this extreme. Then came another shocking revelation: Mackenzie had actually converted to Islam a few months back, but he didn't know if I knew that or not. Apparently the mosque she was attending had assigned her a mentor, who was teaching her how to be a good Muslim wife, so they knew the marriage was being planned and were supporting it. Jeff knew the first name of the guy Mack was evidently engaged to marry and that he lived in Kosovo. Finally, Jeff outlined the dangers he knew about in that part of the world, including human trafficking. After Jeff and I talked for twenty or thirty minutes, we wrapped up the call. He told me he was praying for us and that he had no idea what to tell me to do, other than we needed to take possession of her passport right away. I was extremely grateful for the phone calls and information shared with me by Scot and Jeff. I know that these were not easy conversations for them, but it showed great friendship and courage. I was also keenly aware that the biggest heroes were their daughters, who came forward and told their fathers what was happening, because they trusted their dads and they loved Mackenzie.

After talking with Jeff, I lingered in the park for another half hour, as I processed everything that had happened. Nothing was the same now. My priorities were completely turned around. Mackenzie's life was in grave danger, and we had two weeks to figure out how to save her. The problem was that Mackenzie didn't want to be saved. She wanted to leave us, but at least we now knew what was really going on.

> Mackenzie's life was in grave danger, and we had two weeks to figure out how to save her.

Fortunately, the truth shines light on what is hidden in the dark. Now that her secrets could be seen, action could be taken. *But what could I do?* I got up and headed back inside. I needed to call Stephanie. She would need me to be strong, and I wasn't there yet.

I learned long ago that God helps us in many ways. In my time of crisis, He sent a new friend to me in my darkest hour. As I returned to the meeting room, Cindy was ending the conference call, so I sat back down. She asked if I was okay. I shook my head no, but told her it was going to be all right. As I was speaking, Lisa, a bank executive whom I worked with closely, walked into the room. Lisa looked at me with concern and asked if everything was okay. Cindy got up and left the room, shutting the door behind her, as Lisa sat down next to me.

"What's wrong, John?" she asked me.

Grief-stricken, I quietly told Lisa what I had just learned about Mackenzie. Lisa listened intently, and compassionately set aside her bank position and title to talk with me as a friend. She asked thoughtful questions about what I knew and didn't know. She shared her faith in Christ, and told me how we must hold on to that faith in our times of greatest turmoil. Then she shared with me her own personal story of rebellion against her family. She encouraged me not to turn away from Mackenzie, because her own personal experience was that she finally reconciled with her parents, who continued to love her despite her mistakes.

Lisa's words were exactly what I needed to hear. They were words of hope, words of healing, words of love, and words of friendship. God's grace shone on me in that hour through a bank executive I had only known for a few months. Lisa would tell me later she had no idea why she went to the conference room at that moment. She had been in a meeting and felt compelled to step away to see how things were going. She had not gone down to that room in days. That is God's mercy and grace at work.

As our time together drew to a close, Lisa shifted to the more practical aspects of the situation. "What are you planning to do next?" she asked.

"For now, all I know to do is get her passport and figure out a way to stop her," I answered.

After some reflection, Lisa asked if I thought there was any way to get the authorities involved. She pointed out that this man may be taking advantage of an American citizen in order to do her harm.

"Maybe, if you could convince Homeland Security or the FBI that her life was in danger, you could make a case for them to help," she suggested.

I hadn't thought about anything like that, but it sure sounded good to me. What did I have to lose? And right then, it seemed like our only hope in saving Mackenzie.

When I returned to the hotel that evening, I called Stephanie and told her what I'd learned. Shocked, devastated, and betrayed, she went through the same emotions and reactions I'd experienced only a few hours earlier.

I asked Stephanie to get Mackenzie's passport and hide it. We decided that we needed to keep the information a strict secret from everyone. Jeff and Scot had warned us that if Mackenzie believed we knew about her plan, she would leave the country immediately. At that moment, the only advantage we had was that we knew what she was planning to do, and she didn't know that we knew. We had to keep what we'd learned a secret until we figured out what to do next.

The next morning, I awoke to the reality that time was against us. I had an early breakfast with my three managers—Sam, Jackie, and J.D., a good friend of almost thirty years. They looked at me in disbelief when I laid out the story and told them I needed to focus on my family for a while. It was no surprise when they told me, "Don't worry about work. We'll take care of it." When I mentioned that I hoped to get the authorities involved, Jackie volunteered to contact a friend of hers who worked for the FBI and put him in touch with me. Sam told me that if that didn't work, he knew "a special ops guy" in Florida who specialized in handling problems, particularly those that involved people overseas. If things didn't go anywhere through official channels, Sam thought he could put me in touch with him. Looking back, it was a little humorous to talk about contacting a covert agent, but I swear I would have done it. Whatever I had to do to save Mackenzie, I would do.

> Looking back, it was a little humorous to talk about contacting a covert agent, but I swear I would have done it.

When I flew back to Dallas, my mind was racing. Throughout my flight, I was thinking, praying, thinking, and praying some more. I was glad to get home and see Stephanie. I knew we needed each other now more than ever. We were about to face the biggest challenge of our lives, but at least we were in it together, and that was the only thing that felt good.

If there were any lingering doubts as to what was happening, they were eliminated when the mother of one of Mackenzie's best friends contacted Stephanie the next Saturday and confirmed everything we had been told earlier in the week. Her daughter, Madison, had many more details she wanted to share with us. We later learned that Madison told her mom she wouldn't be able to live with herself if something happened to Mackenzie and felt she had to do something.

The information Madison's mother shared with us was heartbreaking and enlightening, as we learned the depth of the deception that had been woven over the past several months. For example, Mackenzie had even changed Aadam's name to Miriam in her phone. For weeks, she had been telling us she was "talking to Miriam" about the trip to Switzerland, but she was really talking to Aadam.

Even more alarming, Madison confirmed Mackenzie had indeed converted to Islam, kept Islamic clothing in her car, and that she was regularly visiting a mosque and meeting with an Islamic family, who was teaching her how to become a "good Muslim wife." Madison even provided us the name of the girl who had agreed to drive Mackenzie to the airport on the day she was supposed to leave, and the excuse she was planning to use to get away from the house that weekend. Madison knew the full name of the man Mack was involved with and knew he lived in Kosovo and was Albanian. She texted us screenshots of his Facebook page and screenshots of Islamic postings Mackenzie had placed on her page.

Most importantly, Madison had knowledge that Mackenzie was likely planning to leave for Kosovo as early as Wednesday, June 11—the day after her graduation ceremonies—but definitely before our planned vacation to Mexico in early July. This news came as a huge relief because it gave us at least two more weeks than we originally thought we had. Madison continued to provide us with extremely valuable information in the following days. Without her help, it would have been impossible for us to put a plan into action. One thing was for sure: the clock was ticking and we didn't have much time.

CHAPTER 15

Cat and Mouse

John

When we finally figured out what was going on with Mackenzie, Stephanie and I entered into a private promise that no matter what happened, we were not going to allow anything to impact our relationship. During our twenty-nine-year marriage, Stephanie and I had always approached things together. We communicated with each other, respected each other's talents and strengths, and most importantly trusted each other implicitly.

Of course, we did not want what was happening to our daughter to be true, but we had no doubt that it was. Once we talked it through, we began to see how the pieces fit together. We were gripped with fear, but at least we finally knew the truth behind our year of turmoil—Aadam. Why Mackenzie was converting to Islam, her separation from friends and family, and her relentless pursuit to save money snapped into place and made sense now.

Thomas Kuhn, the renowned American physicist, historian,

and philosopher, has called what was happening to us a "paradigm shift." Once the truth was finally revealed to us, the events of the past were seen from their true perspective. We thought Mackenzie's shift toward Islam was about religion, but now we knew there was a love interest behind it.

A quick Google search revealed that Kosovo and countries in the Baltic region were extraordinarily poor—in the bottom 2 percent of the world. Kosovo was still struggling to recover economically from the bloody Kosovo War of 1998–99, which was part of the wider regional Yugoslav Wars. Kosovo was known for human trafficking, sex trafficking, and organized crime. The country's population of 2.2 million was made up of mostly Albanians and much fewer Serbs, and more than 95 percent of the people were Muslim, according to census figures.

Stephanie and I agreed that we had to assume Mackenzie was being manipulated and that she was in grave danger. Now secrecy was of the utmost importance. We could not tell a soul what was going on, including Stephanie's parents, who were living with us under the same roof. We couldn't even give them a hint that something was wrong. We had to carry on about our days and figure out what to do without anyone knowing what we were doing. We had a little bit of time to stop her from leaving. It was less than a month, but at least it was something.

Even now, years later, I still struggle to find the words to describe what we were feeling at the time. At first Stephanie and I were in shock. We struggled to comprehend what our daughter was trying to do and why she would want to do it. *She would really buy an airline ticket, board a plane, and leave us without even saying good-bye? She honestly would leave everything in her life for a guy she had never met in person? She would rather live in a third world country as a Muslim housewife? She would do that to us? She would do that to her brothers?*

John, Stephanie, and Dr. George Mason at Mackenzie's baby dedication ceremony in January 1996, when her life verse was read to her for the first time.
BALDWIN FAMILY

John and Mackenzie playing "horsey" in 1996.
BALDWIN FAMILY

John and Mackenzie in 1998, next to the clock bearing her initials on the pendulum and her life verse—2 Corinthians 9:15—at the base. It still hangs in their home today and was there, faithfully counting the seconds, during the meeting with the FBI.
BALDWIN FAMILY

Mackenzie on a YMCA father-daughter camp-out in 2001.
BALDWIN FAMILY

Mackenzie and Stephanie on a surprise trip to Disney World for Mackenzie's kindergarten graduation in May 2002.
BALDWIN FAMILY

Mackenzie was quite the daredevil. At nine years old, she rode her four-wheeler around the family cabin in Oklahoma, showing off sliding stops and figure eights in 2005.
BALDWIN FAMILY

John and Mackenzie on a HATS rock-climbing and camping trip in 2007.
BALDWIN FAMILY

Luke and Mackenzie enjoying the Florida ocean in the summer of 2007.
BALDWIN FAMILY

Mackenzie and her cat, Angel, had a special bond. (2008)
BALDWIN FAMILY

Rock-climbing on a HATS camp-out in Colorado in 2011.
BALDWIN FAMILY

Mackenzie after reaching the summit of a Colorado mountain with her father in 2011.
BALDWIN FAMILY

In Texas tradition, the homecoming mum exchange is a highlight of the school dances. This is the mum James gave Mackenzie in 2012.
BALDWIN FAMILY

Michael backpacking in 2013.
BALDWIN FAMILY

Luke never gets enough of the inner tube. The family spent many days on area lakes during the hot Texas summer of 2013.
BALDWIN FAMILY

This passport photo is from Mackenzie's replacement passport she secured in May 2014, just weeks before she was to leave. Her solemn face and expressionless eyes capture the facade she had been presenting for months.
BALDWIN FAMILY

A letter from Aadam found in the search of Mackenzie's room. Agent El-Sayed noted that it shows an unusually strong command of the English language—a sign, to him, that something was not right.
BALDWIN FAMILY

Dear my sweetie girl, you surprised me that how you changed your life. I'm sure that your heart now is amazing, in the right way. I'll never forget what you did for your life and for me also, because is something that comes inside of you. I know sometimes it's hard for you but not for your heart, cuz it's Allah who protects you and make you strong all the time.

Thank you for your smile, your care and especially your love ♥ Inshe'Allah we will have a great life in future :***

Hey Sweetheart,
well, I am going to try to write better so you can read this ☺
Im so excited for our life hun, we are so close and I just know Im so safe with you. I want to say so much to you, but I want to see your face and hug you when I say it.
You are the closest I have ever been with someone, and I know we will be amazing.
Also, I wanted to thank you honey. I know it was not easy to show me the right way, but you never gave up on me, and you showed me love. Its more than I ever imagined ☺ oh, my hand writing get messy because I wrote too fast sorry.
Even more, your love for Allah is so beautiful and inspiring. I will be like you one day im sure. I want to know everything, and I want to do all things in the right way, I know I dont do all things good, but I am getting better.
Also, I want to say this again, even though I already told you, thank you hun I know this wasn't easy for you either, but you showed me how I should be, and you have so much patients with me. I always will with you.
So this is our first letter ☺
And baby, we will have amazing times soon. I cant wait to finally be in your arms. I'll always be with you.
One one to dua ♥
From: Mackenzie Baldwin

A letter from Mackenzie for Aadam. Stephanie and John's lingering doubts about their daughter's intentions were erased upon finding it.
BALDWIN FAMILY

John and Mackenzie at her high school graduation on June 10, 2014, almost a week after the FBI intervention. She and Aadam were still talking, but it was out in the open. In this picture, they look happy, but it was still a very tense time.
BALDWIN FAMILY

This was taken in July 2014, just weeks after Mack broke things off with Aadam. Finally a happy family again!
BALDWIN FAMILY

Mackenzie in the fall of 2014 with her green-winged macaw, Indy, that she purchased after he was abandoned by his original owner.
BALDWIN FAMILY

Mackenzie's Christmas gift to her parents in 2014.
BALDWIN FAMILY

Aadam always warned Mackenzie not to skydive, despite her passion. After ending it with Aadam, she got her skydiving license in March 2016 and has done almost fifty solo jumps.
BALDWIN FAMILY

Mackenzie and Special Agent Sheridan, whom she personally thanked in August 2016.
BALDWIN FAMILY

From left to right: Jordyn, Mackenzie, Madison, and Sarah, the friends who stepped forward when they realized Mackenzie was in danger. All four girls came together for the first time after Mackenzie's close call when this photograph was taken in May 2017.
BALDWIN FAMILY

John and Mackenzie.
KORI PEARSON

Stephanie, Mackenzie, and John.
KORI PEARSON

The Baldwin family. From left to right: Luke, Stephanie, Mackenzie, John, and Michael.
KORI PEARSON

Obviously, it overwhelmed us to think about. We were consumed by fear for her. It was so easy for us to visualize scenarios in which she was being taken away into a radicalized Muslim unit. Or that someone she wasn't expecting was going to meet her at the airport in Kosovo, take her U.S. passport, and then they could do anything they wanted to her. It felt exactly like the story line from the movie *Taken*, starring Liam Neeson, in which Albanian human traffickers kidnapped his daughter and her friend for sex slavery while they were traveling in France. That movie had a happy ending, but many stories like it in real life don't end well.

We were aware that sex trafficking was a worldwide epidemic that was only getting worse. The International Labour Organization estimates that there are 20.9 million victims of human trafficking globally. Of those, 68 percent are trapped in forced labor, 26 percent are children, and 55 percent are women and girls. These victims are trapped in sexual exploitation, in which their captors use violence, threats, lies, debt bondage, and other forms of coercion to force adults and children to engage in commercial sex acts against their will. Amnesty International has identified Kosovo as one of the world's hotbeds for human trafficking, and that's where our daughter wanted to go.

> Amnesty International has identified Kosovo as one of the world's hotbeds for human trafficking, and that's where our daughter wanted to go.

Mackenzie had always viewed herself as being worldly and streetwise, but the reality was she was raised in Plano, Texas, and had lived a rather sheltered life. As I imagined what could potentially happen to her if she left, I could feel the dread and grief rise up in my throat. I still didn't know what we were going to do to prevent her from leaving, but I knew if things went badly, we didn't want to look back and regret not having done everything we could to save her.

Of course, our first reaction was to come down on her like a hammer on a nail. We could put a complete stop to the entire thing if we confronted her immediately. It didn't take us long to build a timed list of actions that would stop Mackenzie cold in her tracks, at least for a little while: secure her passport, sweep her bank account, move her car to an unknown location, shut off her phone, and change the Wi-Fi password in our house. We knew we could complete this full action list in about fifteen minutes' time. Stephanie and I rehearsed the list several times, carefully thinking through the sequence, timing, and procedures that would be required.

As we considered the plan, it was easy for me to imagine being the "conquering hero," in which I defeated Islamic radicals who stormed our house to get her. But there was so much more in play and at stake. It was obvious that she had been building to this moment for a long time. She had been adamantly defending Islam for months, and now we knew she had gone to extraordinary lengths to keep her plans to leave secret. She *wanted* to leave. We might stop her from going this time, but how many more times would she try to leave? Eventually she would find a way to run away and get where she wanted to go.

In our minds, we had two big problems. Without question, the most important thing we had to do was stop Mackenzie from leaving right then. But the more serious problem—and the more difficult solution to figure out—was how to eliminate her *desire* to leave. How could we change what was in her heart and mind? How could we convince her that it wasn't safe to go there? How could we convince her that she really didn't know this man who may be trying to harm her? We didn't know the answers to those important questions yet; but for now, her immediate safety was of greatest importance.

Stephanie and I knew that our first priority was securing her passport. A few weeks earlier, Mackenzie had asked us for her passport, saying she needed it for work. It was an odd request, and we challenged her on it. Mack told us she didn't know why they needed it, but her manager said he wanted to have multiple forms of identification or something like that. We didn't understand why it was needed, but there wasn't any reason not to give it to her. Now we had to get it back from her without raising suspicion.

Fortunately, we had a long-planned family trip to Mexico coming up in about six weeks that could provide cover. That evening, Stephanie casually told her that she wanted to get our passports together so we wouldn't lose track of them before the trip. She had noticed Mack hadn't returned hers after taking it to work. Stephanie asked Mackenzie to get the passport for her, and, much to our surprise and relief, she ran upstairs to get it for us. Stephanie took our passports and placed them in our safe-deposit box at the bank, and we felt like we had taken a major step in blocking Mack's ability to leave the country.

Our next immediate goal was to limit Mackenzie's ability to purchase an airline ticket—if she didn't already have one. Mack had been relentlessly working and saving money for months under the pretense of paying for her trip to Switzerland, and we knew she had accumulated more than $6,000. Another piece of the puzzle clicked into place. Two months earlier, Mackenzie insisted on having a new checking account opened in her name only and wanted to close a joint account she shared with Stephanie. After a long discussion, Stephanie agreed to let her open a new account. But at the last second, by some small miracle, Stephanie suggested they keep the joint account open with five dollars in it, so she would be able to move money to Mackenzie's personal account in the event of an emergency.

We knew there was more than enough money in Mackenzie's personal account to purchase a plane ticket to Kosovo. Later that night, Stephanie pulled up Mack's bank account and realized the private account and joint account were linked, allowing us the ability to move funds from one account to the other. It also provided us access to monitor the transactions and activity in Mack's personal account. Stephanie noticed an April 2014 transaction with Planned Parenthood, and after a quick call she learned it was the exact amount required to purchase birth control pills. We were relieved to not find a large purchase for airline tickets. It was obviously a positive sign, but we also realized the guy overseas might have purchased a ticket for her.

Shortly afterward, Jackie emailed me the name of an FBI agent based in Charlotte who agreed to talk to me. I immediately reached out to him by phone. The agent was sympathetic, very concerned, and agreed that Mackenzie could easily be walking into a highly dangerous situation. He told me that this kind of situation was not his area of expertise, but he had a fellow agent based in Dallas who might be able to help us. He said he would work to put us in touch with each other.

Stephanie and I were feeling the personal strain and stress about what Mackenzie was planning—and even more so, our inability to do much about it. We decided to talk to Pastor Sam, our pastor at Parkway Hills Baptist Church, because we knew that perhaps no one is better at finding the right words, the right prayer, and the right tone to help others through difficult times. Despite the obvious seriousness of the situation, Stephanie and I had to chuckle when I said that our crisis was probably going to be a first, even for Pastor Sam.

That morning, May 15, Sam welcomed Stephanie and me into his office, and the three of us sat together in a small circle in front of his desk. Sam knew that Mackenzie had been pulling away from the church and her family and friends, and he was aware of her interest in Islam. But nothing could have prepared him for the bombshell we dropped on him that morning. Once we told Sam what was happening, he did not offer any promises or potential solutions. But he reminded us of Christ's unending love for Mackenzie and us, and encouraged us

> **Stephanie and I were feeling the personal strain and stress about what Mackenzie was planning—and our inability to do much about it.**

to lean on Him for strength and wisdom. Sam also made it a point to tell us that we needed to remember our sons, Michael and Luke, during this difficult time, and that we shouldn't lose sight of our responsibility for their care, safety, and well-being.

After listening to Sam for twenty minutes or so, I finally asked him what had been on my mind the past few weeks. I was a deacon in the church, and I had taken a pledge to raise my family under the guidance of Jesus Christ and keep my house in spiritual order. It was obvious to me that I had not kept that pledge, so I asked Sam if it would be best if we changed churches or withdrew from some of the ministries in which we were involved. He would hear nothing of it and told us that everyone has problems—everyone. Sam advised us to keep Jesus front and center and continue loving Mackenzie. Sam then looked at me and firmly told me that I needed to be strong for my wife, daughter, and boys. It was what I needed to hear, and I nodded with him in agreement. We prayed together, holding hands, and he gave us a big hug before we left.

Stephanie and I drove home without any new answers, but we

felt stronger. We had no idea what we were going to do, but we were praying for doors to open, for wisdom, and for strength. At that very moment, we had nothing.

The next morning, when Mackenzie came downstairs for school, she asked Stephanie for her passport back. It was the first time we had witnessed her putting her plan to leave into action, and it hurt deeply. Somehow, Stephanie remained poised as she explained to Mack that she had given it to her once for her job and didn't see any reason for her to have it again. We noticed a visible flash of concern in Mackenzie's eyes when she realized she wasn't going to get her passport back. She protested loudly that her boss needed it, but Stephanie told her if her manager needed it that badly, he could call her directly. Mackenzie was angry, but she uncharacteristically dropped the subject and left. Later that night, she asked Stephanie for the passport again, this time saying she wanted to show it to her friend Miriam. Stephanie once again refused to give it to her.

That afternoon, Stephanie noticed a financial transaction come across Mackenzie's personal account. It was an odd amount— $184.85—and we couldn't figure out what it was for. It certainly wasn't enough to pay for a plane ticket to Eastern Europe, and we hadn't noticed that Mack had made any other big purchases. With the clock ticking toward her planned departure date, we didn't have very long to figure out what it was for.

CHAPTER 16

Alarming Discoveries

John

On Sunday, May 18, Stephanie and I celebrated our twenty-ninth wedding anniversary. Obviously, with everything that was happening, it wasn't much of a celebration. Five days after finding out about Mackenzie's plan, we were relieved that she was still at home and wasn't on the other side of the world. That morning, I drove to the church early because I had morning greeter duties. Stephanie arrived shortly after with all three kids. We tried to keep it as much of a typical Sunday morning as possible.

After Sunday school began, Stephanie circled back to our house and did a thorough search of Mackenzie's bedroom. To ensure everything would be placed back exactly the way it was found, she took several photographs of Mack's room. She found a handwritten letter from Aadam in an envelope addressed to Mackenzie at a P.O. box, a letter she had written to him but not yet mailed, and a padded yellow envelope dated February 19 that was addressed to his

Kosovo address, but had been returned. Four Islamic books were hidden under Mack's mattress. She found more books, several hajibs, and other articles of clothing hidden in Mackenzie's car.

Unfortunately, she didn't find anything that provided us with further details about Mack's travel plans, but at least we now had the guy's physical address in Kosovo. Finding out Mackenzie had secretly rented a P.O. box was yet another disappointment and a sign of the level of sophistication in her efforts to deceive us. She returned to the church less than an hour later, and by some small miracle was able to park in the same parking spot, avoiding potential questions.

That Sunday afternoon, we called our longtime friends Steve and Shelly Francis and asked if we could come over to talk with them. At the time, Steve was working as the senior safety manager at Dallas/Fort Worth International Airport. He had spent a long time working in security, including many years in the Middle East, and was very knowledgeable in certain areas of law enforcement. Shelly is a deeply spiritual woman, who is quick to sustain friends in need with loving-kindness and prayer. They were exactly who we needed to talk with.

As we told them our story about Mackenzie that night, they could only shake their heads in disbelief. Having known our daughter since she was two years old, it was hard for them to comprehend what they heard. In her gentle way, Shelly offered scripture and words of hope and strength. Steve, always measured and cerebral in his responses, didn't say much at first as he considered the situation. He asked us a few questions about details, and then told us what he knew about Kosovo—including sex trafficking, money scams, and money fraud. He offered to talk to the Dallas/Fort Worth Airport chief of police, Charles Cinquemani, about our situation in the event things didn't pan out with the Charlotte- and Dallas-based

FBI guys I was currently trying to get to help us. Steve said he would ask him what the rules were for flagging passports at Dallas/Fort Worth Airport and see if he had any other ideas on what to do to prevent her from boarding a plane. At the end of the evening, we prayed together for Mackenzie's well-being and for doors to open so we could save her. Our friends had given us a new sense of hope, a word of affirmation, and the loving support that good friends give.

That night, at about two o'clock early Monday morning, Stephanie awoke with a start. She sat up in bed, grabbed my arm, and said, "Oh, my God, John. She doesn't have to reapply for a passport. She could order a replacement. That's what the money was for!" We had wrongly assumed that when we took Mackenzie's passport from her, it would take her many weeks to get a new one. Stephanie turned on a bedroom lamp, opened her laptop, and went to the U.S. State Department's website. Sure enough, much to our dismay, the fees for a replacement passport and birth certificate, with expedited delivery, totaled exactly $184.85. Now things were different. We knew Mack had a P.O. box, but we couldn't find the key for it, and we assumed her replacement passport would be sent there. Once the new passport arrived, she would be able to leave the country at any time. We had to find the P.O. box key and take the passport before she retrieved it.

> We prayed together for Mackenzie's well-being and for doors to open so we could save her.

Tuesday, May 20, marked one week since we'd learned about Mackenzie's plans, but it felt like it had been a month. We calculated that if the passport was expedited, it would probably arrive sometime Tuesday or Wednesday, and we were deeply worried. When I talked to the Dallas-based FBI agent, he told me he was willing to help, but was currently deeply involved with another case and couldn't talk to me for a few days. I wasn't going to wait that long. I placed a call to Steve and asked if he'd reach out to the Dallas/Fort Worth Airport chief of police. Steve said he'd let me know when he had talked to him.

As the days slowly passed, the stress mounted. The need for us to maintain absolute secrecy in a crowded house made things worse. It would have been hard enough with only our boys, but with Stephanie's parents also living there, it complicated things greatly. Strangely enough, our attached rear garage became the best place for us to talk freely, take phone calls, or simply console each other. Multiple times a day, one of us would catch the eye of the other, and we'd make our way to the garage separately and rendezvous there to give each other updates or simply comfort each other for a few minutes. Then we'd collect ourselves and try to go back to acting normally with everyone else. Fortunately, our managers at work had given us time off to deal with the emergency, and since we both regularly worked from home, it wasn't a red flag to Mackenzie that we were there so much.

Stephanie and I spent every available minute tracking down any lead in an attempt to obtain specific information about Mackenzie's plan to leave, how we could stop her, or how we might change her mind. Amazingly, no one in our busy house ever knew a single detail about what we knew or what we were doing until we were ready to let them know.

Every night, when Mackenzie's midnight curfew rolled around, we tried to remain calm, especially when Stephanie's parents were in the room with us. Unbeknownst to them, we were being torn apart with worry until the door opened and she walked in. We made frequent drive-bys past her workplace to make sure her car was still there. One night, as we lay awake in bed in our guest bedroom that is positioned next door to Mackenzie's room (Stephanie's parents were sleeping in our master bedroom), we finally relented to a wave of fear, dread, worry, and, a complete sense of failure as parents. We held each other and sobbed as if Mackenzie had died. We dealt with the crisis together and took care never to blame each other for anything that had gone wrong. Concerns with her Islamic conversion, once paramount, were now secondary to her safety and well-being.

Most of all, we viewed our current crisis as a fight for Mackenzie's life, and we were going to fight for her whether she wanted us to or not. At the end of the day, we accepted that our efforts might indeed fail, and that she might one day soon find herself in Kosovo or in a dangerous trap that threatened her life. But for Mackenzie to get there, she was going to have to overcome everything we had. Win or lose, we were determined to leave no stone unturned and no possibility unchecked. No matter what ultimately happened, we wanted no regrets and no second thoughts. We knew we were fighting for Mack's life.

Without knowing when her replacement passport would be delivered, it was extremely important that we maintained secrecy until we figured out what to do. Meanwhile, the charade at home continued to play out. Mackenzie came and left our house as usual, seemingly only worried about finishing high school. Luke and Michael went about their days in their normal activities. My in-laws continued to battle Stephanie's father's health problems. Since Stephanie and I worked from home, it was possible for us to pretend to work, but in reality every conversation and action we took was part of the secret war we were silently fighting. It took great restraint to maintain our composure, and we blamed the times we cracked on our concern for Stephanie's father. That appeased the kids, including Mackenzie.

> No matter what ultimately happened, we wanted no regrets and no second thoughts. We were fighting for Mack's life.

On Wednesday, May 21, Steve called to follow up on the offer he'd made Sunday to call Charles Cinquemani, the Dallas/Fort Worth Airport chief of police. He said he'd had a five-minute conversation with Charles and told him what was happening with Mackenzie. Chief Cinquemani said that, unfortunately, there was nothing the airport could do to flag Mackenzie's passport, since she was eighteen. His primary concern, he said, was that Mackenzie may have gotten involved with a jihad recruitment or was unknowingly caught up in a human trafficking operation. He asked for, and Steve provided, Mackenzie's name and my phone number. At the end of the meeting, Chief Cinquemani told Steve, "Let me see what I can do. Tell them that if they do get a call from the FBI, it will be from an agent stationed at Dallas/Fort Worth Airport."

I hung up the phone and felt a wave of emotion that brought tears to my eyes. Finally, we were close to getting help from someone with the authority to block Mack's passport and maybe even convince her of the danger she was walking into. The sequence of events up until now was so inexplicable that we could only thank God. Now, if someone from the FBI would only call us back. My daughter was leaving for Kosovo in a matter of days, and we were running out of time.

Mackenzie

Once I knew I'd be leaving the country to go meet Aadam, I started planning for my trip. I read everything I could find about traveling abroad. I'd never spent much time on an airplane; I'd never even flown out of the United States. But now I was preparing to fly around the world to a country and region I knew absolutely nothing about.

Of course, I knew I wouldn't get anywhere if I didn't have my passport. I knew my mom kept our passports in a drawer in the desk in my dad's office. About once a week, I'd go downstairs in the middle of the night to check the drawer to make sure the passports were still there. As my date of departure drew closer, I checked the drawer more frequently. About two months before my trip, I was even checking every night. At one point, I had asked Mom for my passport, claiming I needed it for work. I kept it in my room after that, but eventually she asked for it back. I assumed she would put it back in the desk drawer.

A couple of nights later, I went downstairs after everyone else was asleep, like I normally did, and opened the drawer. But when I opened the drawer the passports were gone! I couldn't believe it, and my heart started racing. I was overcome by anxiety, and I felt my chest tighten. I could hardly breathe. *No passport, no Aadam*, I thought. I quietly closed the desk drawer and ran back upstairs to my room. My first step was to find out where the passports were. I figured my parents had done something with them in preparation for our family trip to Cancún, Mexico, that summer. I tried to fall asleep that night, but couldn't. I knew I had to wait to ask my parents about my passport, and I knew I had to do it matter-of-factly so they wouldn't be alarmed.

By the time morning arrived, I had a plan in place. My parents knew I was flying to Switzerland that summer to see my friend Miriam. I figured I could simply tell my parents that Miriam and I were comparing our passports, and I wanted to show mine to her. It seemed like a plausible request, and then hopefully I'd find out where my mom was now keeping them. I walked downstairs to ask for my passport, trying to look as calm and normal as possible.

"Hey, Mom, Miriam and I were talking last night and she showed me her passport," I said. "I wanted to show her mine but couldn't find it. Do you have any idea where it is?"

My mom didn't look up, and she was very hard to read.

"We moved them to the safe-deposit box at the bank so they would be safe, since we're leaving for Mexico in a couple of months," she said.

Of course, I knew I couldn't get access to their safe-deposit box, and I was frantic. I went upstairs, opened my laptop, and started researching how to obtain a new passport. I went to the mosque later that day, and I asked Hadiya if she knew anything I could do. She told me I could file an application for a replacement passport and say my original was lost; it was a quicker and less expensive process than ordering a new one. Hadiya knew my parents didn't know about Aadam, but I hadn't been completely honest with her either. I told her that I met him during a trip to Europe that I'd taken with my family. I told her we'd only spent a day together, but had been talking ever since.

> I felt bad lying to Hadiya, but that's all I seemed to do now. It was exhausting trying not to get caught in the tangled web I'd weaved.

I felt bad lying to Hadiya, but that's all I seemed to do now. It was exhausting trying not to get caught in the tangled web I'd weaved to cover my tracks. Now I was about to commit another act of deception. I figured obtaining a replacement passport was a foolproof plan, and I was going to file the application for one the next day.

CHAPTER 17

A Father's Love

John

Finally, on Thursday, May 22, the call we had desperately been waiting for came. FBI Special Agent Kevin Sheridan contacted me, and asked that Stephanie and I meet him at his office at Dallas/Fort Worth International Airport. We agreed to meet the next morning.

As Stephanie and I drove to Dallas/Fort Worth Airport on Friday morning, we talked about what we hoped to get out of the conference. First we agreed that we wanted the FBI to confiscate Mackenzie's passport, or at least put her on a no-fly list to block her from leaving the country. We also hoped the FBI agents would talk to Mack about the dangers she was placing herself in, which we hoped would persuade her not to want to go to Kosovo. When we reached the FBI office, which was located away from the expansive airline terminals, Agent Sheridan opened his office door and invited us into a small conference room to talk. Agent Sheridan looked to be about my age, probably in his fifties, and he was slightly taller than me. He was wearing a dark suit and tie with a small FBI pin affixed to his lapel. He certainly looked like an FBI agent. One of Agent Sheridan's colleagues was also sitting at the small round table with us.

Agent Sheridan started the interview by telling us that he'd received information that our daughter might be involved in a relationship with someone overseas, apparently a Muslim, and that she was considering leaving the country to be with him. Since Agent Sheridan didn't know many of the details, he wanted us to tell him everything we knew so he could assess whether anything was happening that might constitute a crime. I spent several minutes telling the FBI agents what we knew about Mackenzie's relationship with Aadam, and then I shared with them the letters we found in her bedroom. I told them that we knew she'd sent him a couple of packages and had a secret P.O. box, and I also showed them screenshots of his Facebook page. I held what I hoped was the most convincing argument for last. I told them she had ordered an expedited replacement passport after we'd taken possession of her original. At this point, the best estimate we had was that she planned to leave for Kosovo sometime between June 11 and before our planned vacation in early July.

Sheridan and the other FBI agent took expansive notes as Stephanie and I told them everything we knew about Aadam, and then they asked a series of probing follow-up questions. Among them: What did she mail to him? What were the names of the authors of the Islamic books she was reading? What were the names of the imams she was watching online? Had the man in Kosovo contacted anyone else in our family? Was Mackenzie involved with drugs or having any trouble at school? What was her personality like? What was her relationship like with us at home? Did she have any friends? How did we find out about her money and bank account? Did we know if she was attending a mosque? And, finally, had she ever said anything that suggested a radical Islamic point of view?

When Stephanie and I told them the names of the imams who were featured in the Islamic videos that Mackenzie had been watching online, Sheridan told us that they were zealous in their Islamic teachings and were involved in aggressively recruiting followers to the religion, but he didn't think they were radical or violent, and they were not generally regarded as a threat. Sheridan and the other agent told us they each had extensive experience with Islam from working in the Middle East, so they were well acquainted with signs of radicalization. Sheridan, who'd worked in law enforcement for nearly two decades, was the aviation liaison agent coordinator at the FBI Dallas Field Office. He was responsible for managing FBI security and investigative operations at Dallas/Fort Worth International Airport, including criminal, counterterrorism, and counterintelligence. He had previously been a supervisory special agent in the FBI Dallas Field Office, where he managed an international terrorism squad tasked with targeting terrorist organizations with connections to the United States and its allies, and he was also a former U.S. Army officer. In summary, he was exactly the kind of guy we needed on Mackenzie's case.

Sheridan asked us if Mackenzie understood the part of the world where she wanted to go and a woman's role in Muslim society. The agents outlined their personal experiences with women being treated oppressively and sometimes violently. Sheridan said living in Kosovo was much different from how women lived in Texas. In the Middle East, women sometimes have to sit outside restaurants, while their husbands go inside to eat. They're mostly responsible for household chores and raising children. Sheridan told us that while Kosovo is notorious for sex trafficking, human trafficking, organ harvesting, citizenship fraud, and money scams, it was not known for being radically Islamic.

Sheridan then asked us more specific questions about Mackenzie's passport. We told him that once we'd taken her original passport, we noticed the financial transaction for an expedited replacement. Sheridan explained that Mackenzie's actions might be considered passport fraud under federal law, but the offense was rarely enforced on its own. Since I was desperately searching for any way for authorities to stop her from leaving the United States, I told the FBI agents that I'd be in favor of them arresting her for passport fraud if necessary. I told them I'd rather have her alive in jail than dead overseas, but Sheridan didn't acknowledge my request.

> I told them I'd rather have her alive in jail than dead overseas, but Sheridan didn't acknowledge my request.

After talking with us for about thirty minutes, Sheridan closed the meeting by telling us he didn't see anything at the moment that warranted him opening a criminal case. He said he understood our concerns, but it was really nothing more than an eighteen-year-old woman being involved in a romantic relationship with someone overseas. He didn't see anything criminally wrong with what was going on with Mackenzie, but he did think that how their relationship started and their plans for her to travel there were suspicious. While Aadam might have fraudulent motives for getting her there, there wasn't any strong evidence of what he might be doing at this point. Sheridan told us the biggest problem we faced was that Mackenzie was eighteen and a legal adult under the law. As an adult, she had legal rights that had to be protected too.

"Look, it's not a crime to be a Muslim," he told us. "There would be far more we could do if she were seventeen, but unfortunately she's not. That said, she is a kid who's still in high school and is putting herself in a dangerous situation with a guy, who more than likely is not in this relationship for love or religion."

Obviously, what Agent Sheridan was saying was not what Stephanie and I wanted to hear. We wanted the FBI to open a criminal case, to confiscate Mackenzie's passport, and to become officially involved in the case and stop her from leaving. I looked at Agent Sheridan and told him, "All I want is to keep her safe. I want to find a way to stop her from going over there and getting hurt or killed. She's my little girl. If it takes arresting her for passport fraud, I don't care. I just want her alive and over here. Even if you guys can just talk to her about what she's getting into, that would help us tremendously. We need to find a way to really put a shock in her to get her off this path. She won't listen to us, but I think she would listen to you.

"Can you put her on a no-fly list?" I asked him.

"No, not without opening a criminal case," he answered. "But there might be some other things we can do."

Sheridan told us that they would look into Aadam's background and that he'd take a closer look at passport laws to see if there was anything they could do. As Stephanie and I prepared to leave, Sheridan told us he would find a way to help. He said he needed to consult with his supervisor to figure out what he might legally be able to do, and he encouraged us to maintain our secrecy for now. Sheridan told me he'd call me with an update.

Although Stephanie and I were disappointed the FBI didn't immediately open a criminal case or put Mackenzie on a no-fly list, we were encouraged that they were going to help us. We were grateful they were willing to listen and become involved, but we were still extremely concerned. If the FBI couldn't stop Mackenzie from leaving, Stephanie and I were going to be on our own, and our chances of stopping her from going to Kosovo were probably slim to none.

I was relieved when Agent Sheridan called the next day to let me know he had spoken to his management and they were checking to see what they could do to assist us. In the meantime, he said I could call him at any time, and he'd be glad to provide any help or advice he could. After the long Memorial Day weekend, I decided to try and work a little bit, but it was extremely difficult to focus for long. It was Tuesday, May 27, and Stephanie needed to leave the house and go to her office for a couple of hours. Soon after she left, I felt the familiar waves of anxiety well up inside me. I envisioned my little girl boarding a plane to Kosovo. Trying to make sense of why she would do this was nearly incapacitating. Knowing that she probably had a replacement passport in hand was deeply troubling. Every time she left the house, I feared it would be the last time I would ever see her. I told my mother-in-law I had to run a few errands, and I jumped in my truck and drove to the church to find Pastor Sam. His office was empty, and his assistant told me he was in the Fellowship Hall. I found him talking with people at a staff breakfast, and when he saw me, he knew immediately that something was wrong. He took my arm and led me out of the room. I couldn't talk and walked next to him with tears streaming down my face.

Pastor Sam led me into the worship center, which was empty, and we sat down in two chairs against the back wall. I broke down and couldn't stop crying; I hadn't cried like that since my dad died. The only thing I could ask Pastor Sam was, "Why? Why is she doing this?" I must have cried for ten minutes, and for the life of me, I couldn't stop. Pastor Sam sat next to me, saying nothing, with his arm around my shoulders. When I finally got most of it out of my system, Sam told me Jesus was going to get us through this crisis.

I shook my head and said I wasn't so sure anymore. I thought we'd be fine at first, but now I didn't know if even Jesus was going to be enough. She wanted to leave. Mackenzie was almost gone.

> I didn't know if even Jesus was going to be enough. Mackenzie wanted to leave. She was almost gone.

Then Pastor Sam told me something I will never forget. He said, "John, look at me." I raised my head to look at him.

"John, what will bring her back is a Father's love," he said. "Your love for her and the Father's love will bring her home, and you have to remain strong. Your wife and your boys need you to be strong."

With his arm still around my shoulders, Pastor Sam prayed with me. I don't remember exactly what he said, but I felt a renewed strength and focus that the Father's love would bring Mackenzie home. I didn't have another bad day like that again.

CHAPTER 18

A Plan to Save Her

John

I returned home from the church feeling better. Then that afternoon, much to my relief, Agent Sheridan called to check and see how we were doing. That phone call ushered in a partnership for which I will be forever grateful. He and I talked every day that week, even if for only a few minutes. I called him with questions, concerns, or ideas that Stephanie and I had about how to deal with the dire situation. Much of our early discussions were providing him updates on Mackenzie's actions, as well as any additional information we received from her friend Madison or what we could find ourselves. Our primary focus at the time was to find her passport and key to the P.O. box, which we assumed was where her passport was being stored. We were still operating under the assumption that the earliest she was planning to leave was June 11, the day after high school graduation ceremonies—only two weeks away.

We looked everywhere for the P.O. box key and passport. We

searched her room every time she left the house, including her bathroom, closets, desk, under her bed, and even under the toilet lid. When she was asleep we checked her car, but found nothing. The one place we were never able to check was the brown leather messenger bag we'd given her in place of the skydiving trip for her eighteenth birthday. She carried the bag everywhere and never allowed it out of her sight. We became convinced the key had to be in the bag, if we could only get to it.

Then one morning we had a brief opportunity to search the bag. She left it downstairs on the floor while she ran up to her room to retrieve something. Without speaking a word, Stephanie grabbed the bag, and I positioned myself at the bottom of the stairs to signal her when Mack was coming down. Within twenty seconds, I frantically signaled Stephanie. She flipped down the flap on the bag and moved it back to its original place near the sofa, while I turned and walked into my office. Mackenzie grabbed her bag, said good-bye, and left for school. I walked into the living room, and Stephanie shook her head no. She didn't have time to search the entire bag.

That night, I decided to purchase a GPS device and hide it in the back of Mackenzie's car. She'd turned off the "Find My Phone" feature on her iPhone, and it was too risky for us to try to turn it back on. The GPS device would allow us to keep track of her movements at all times.

On Wednesday, May 28, Agent Sheridan called and said he was able to check with most of the airlines that flew out of Dallas/Fort Worth International Airport, and from what he had gathered Mackenzie hadn't purchased an airline ticket and didn't have a reservation for a flight to Kosovo. The revelation gave us tremendous relief, but we knew she could also wait until the last minute to buy a ticket, even up until the day of the flight. She could leave whenever she wanted as long as she had her passport.

During the next few days, we noticed that Mackenzie was spending a little more time at home with her brothers. It became clear to us that she was beginning to realize she was going to be leaving them and wouldn't see them for some time—or even ever again. On one of the nights she was home, I decided to take a chance and talk to her. I knew it was risky, because I didn't want to reveal what Stephanie and I knew about her plans to leave, but it was a chance I decided to take. Once I brought up Islam, Mackenzie rolled her eyes, but seemed willing to talk to me. I remembered what Pastor Sam had told me earlier that week about remaining strong, and I decided to tell Mackenzie about the Parable of the Lost Son from Luke 15:11–31.

"There is a story in the Bible about a guy who lived at home and was very comfortable with his family and possessions, but then he didn't like it and decided he wanted to leave his faith and his family behind, so he left," I told her. "Once he arrived at his new home, he found out that life there was way more difficult than he could have imagined. When he hit rock bottom, he decided he wanted to go back to his family, but he was afraid.

"He wrote a small speech and rehearsed it over and over as to what he was going to say to his dad when he went home. Finally, he got up the courage to go home, and his dad ran out to meet him before he even reached the front gate. As the son started his speech, his father interrupted him in the middle of it and welcomed him back to his family."

Mackenzie looked at me as I shared the parable with her but said nothing. So I continued to talk to her. I needed to remember to love her where she was at and to trust that a father's love would bring her home.

"Mackenzie, I don't know what is going through your head right now," I told her. "I don't understand why you're doing what you're doing, and you know I don't agree with it. But I want you to know something—I am the father in that story. And I feel like you've decided to move to that faraway country looking for something different. I think you've got a lot of people telling you not to trust your family because we don't love you, and that we will reject you because of what you are doing. I want you to know that will never happen.

"There is a gap between us right now, and there is a bridge over that gap. You may choose to blow up that bridge on your side. But I'm telling you now that I will never blow that bridge up on my side. I love you unconditionally, and nothing you do or say will ever change that, and that bridge will always be open on my end. I don't want you to ever doubt it or forget it."

> "I love you unconditionally, and nothing you do or say will ever change that. I don't want you to ever doubt it or forget it."

For the first time in a very long time, I saw a glint of a tear in Mackenzie's eye. She gave me a tight hug and went upstairs.

By Friday, May 30, our search for the passport and key had still turned up nothing, and Stephanie and I hadn't had another opportunity to look in Mackenzie's messenger bag again. I continued to stay in close contact with Agent Sheridan, who confirmed with the U.S. State Department that Mackenzie's replacement passport had indeed been delivered to her P.O. box.

The FBI was still conducting a background check on Aadam, and Agent Sheridan was consulting with his colleagues about how to best confront Mackenzie about the situation. At that moment, Agent Sheridan felt pretty confident that Mack didn't have a plane ticket to Kosovo yet, and we had a GPS on her car to let us know if she was headed toward the airport. Overall, despite our situation, Stephanie and I felt pretty good about where things were.

But then, on the morning of Sunday, June 1, our plan to save Mackenzie from herself almost fell apart. As we prepared for church, Mack was in the shower upstairs, and Stephanie noticed the messenger bag on the floor next to her bed. She took the opportunity to search it and found the passport in a side pocket. Stephanie frantically came downstairs, found me, and asked if we should take it. I didn't know what to do. If we took Mack's passport, she couldn't leave. But if she realized it was missing, we'd have to confront her on the spot about what we knew, without having the help and credibility of the FBI agents behind us. It was an extremely difficult decision and we had only a few minutes to make it.

I called Agent Sheridan on his cell phone, but he didn't answer. Stephanie and I realized we were on our own in deciding what to do. We decided that Mack's safety had to come first and we had to prevent her from leaving. Stephanie ran upstairs and took the passport, right before we heard Mackenzie's shower turn off. Standing in the living room with her passport, I heard my cell phone ring. It was Agent Sheridan. I quickly told him what had just transpired, thinking he would approve. But then he said, "You know, I think you should put it back. We have a plan in mind, and I think it will be okay to let her keep it." I couldn't believe what I'd just heard! He wanted us to give Mackenzie back the passport we'd spent days frantically searching for. *Now what were we going to do?*

I told Stephanie that Agent Sheridan said we needed to put the passport back, but Mackenzie was already back in her room. We decided that I'd call Mack downstairs for some reason, and Stephanie would go upstairs and put the passport back into her bag before she realized it was missing. I yelled upstairs for my daughter and waited for her to respond. I didn't know what I was going to say next. I called her again, and she asked what I needed. "Just come downstairs," I told her. "I need to talk to you!"

Exasperated, Mackenzie hurried down to the landing, as Stephanie quickly moved past her on the stairs going up. "What do you need, Dad?" she asked me.

"I just wanted to see what you're doing after church today," I told her.

As Mackenzie prepared to answer me, I heard a noise in her bedroom. Her head snapped in the direction of the sound, and she turned and raced up the stairs. *This is it—we're busted. It's over.* Much to my amazement, I didn't hear any screaming or protests coming from her room. Then Stephanie came walking down the stairs carrying a bunch of clothes hangers, and I looked at her with a puzzled and confused expression. *What in the world had just happened?* Stephanie mouthed to me: *It's okay.* I met Stephanie in our bedroom, where she told me that she'd put the passport back in the bag. Seconds before Mackenzie walked back into her bedroom, Stephanie had turned toward her closet and began gathering clothes hangers for the laundry.

"It couldn't have been two seconds' difference," Stephanie told me. "If that flap didn't open or close, we'd have been caught for sure. It was like somebody opened it up and closed it for me. I couldn't believe it."

After church, I called Agent Sheridan back and told him about our close encounter, which he found quite humorous. He then told me that he and his colleagues had come up with a plan and were ready to talk to Mackenzie. He was going to bring two fellow FBI agents with him, including Special Agent El-Sayed, an expert in the Islamic religion. Sheridan was confident they could help persuade Mackenzie that the man in Kosovo was misleading her. Additionally, Sheridan told me for the first time that he now believed there was criminal intent based on the facts presented, and that he thought Aadam was leveraging religion to manipulate Mack into a scam or, worse, an even more dangerous trap. Since Mackenzie had fraudulently obtained a replacement passport, the FBI had a path to confront her about her planned trip. Sheridan wanted to use the meeting to shock her about the seriousness of the situation, persuade her to break off her relationship with Aadam, and return her to the trust of her family. The meeting was not going to be designed to turn Mackenzie away from Islam and back to Christianity, and I agreed that his plan was the appropriate way to approach this. Her safety was all that mattered now.

> **Agent Sheridan thought Aadam was leveraging religion to manipulate Mack into a scam or, worse, an even more dangerous trap.**

Agent Sheridan and I agreed that the FBI agents would meet with Mackenzie at our house at ten o'clock in the morning on Friday, June 6, which was four days before her graduation ceremonies at Plano West Senior High School. Finally, after weeks of anxiety and fear, we had a good plan in place.

Then, the very next day, Madison called and told us that Mackenzie had changed her plans and was now planning to leave the weekend *before* graduation, Saturday, June 7, twenty-five days from the day I received that first phone call. I called Agent Sheridan and told him the news, and we quickly decided to move up the intervention to Wednesday morning, June 4.

Agent Sheridan also provided me with a very comforting update: he had contacted the U.S. Immigration and Customs Enforcement office, which agreed to stop Mackenzie and notify him personally if she attempted to board an international flight out of Dallas/Fort Worth International Airport. As an added precaution, he made similar arrangements at all other U.S. international airports by flagging her name in the immigration database.

For the first time in a long time, Stephanie and I finally felt like our daughter was safe. But we also knew our biggest challenge was still in front of us: somehow, we had to eliminate Mackenzie's desire to leave. We were about to take that fight to Mackenzie's doorstep, and we now had plenty of firepower helping us.

CHAPTER 19

Confirmation

Mackenzie

By early June I'd saved enough money for my trip to Kosovo, and I was so excited for what was coming. Finally school was going to be over, and I'd get to meet Aadam for real. I hated lying to my parents and knew they would be extremely hurt when I left. Whenever the subject of our family trip to Mexico came up, I felt such added guilt knowing that I'd be gone by then. Hopefully, they'd forgive me quickly and let me have time to be myself at last. I'd tell them to take my brothers to Mexico and just enjoy it. Aadam and I talked frequently, every day making plans for our coming time together. He was as excited as I was about the trip.

But I was torn between the guilt I felt for my family and the excitement I felt when talking to Aadam about when we'd finally be together. When we talked, I was reminded to not be afraid or doubt what I was doing, even if doubt crept in again when I was away from him. The people at the mosque checked in frequently with me, especially if I missed prayer, and they were excited about my coming trip. The plan was set, and, most of the time, I didn't want to change it. Sometimes I had second thoughts, and fear would creep in, but I was in so deep I couldn't see any way out.

After weeks of going back and forth, I finally made the decision to leave on Saturday, June 7, which was only a week away. The time had come for me to buy my plane ticket. When I went online to get it, I was shocked to see that the price was a whopping $1,500! I went to the mosque to ask Hadiya for help in buying the ticket. I'd never purchased a plane ticket before, and I wanted to make sure I did it right. I figured it might be more complicated if you were buying an international ticket.

> The people at the mosque checked in frequently with me, and they were excited about my coming trip.

I sat down with Hadiya, and she walked me through the process. She made me promise that I'd call her every step of the way, so she would know that I was safe. Once I'd provided the required information to purchase the ticket, I entered my debit card number on the airline's website. Then I sat there for a couple of minutes with my mouse hovering over the "confirm purchase" button. Thoughts were swirling through my head, and I could hardly think straight. *This is it*, I thought. *Was this really what I wanted to do? Was it the right thing to do?*

I had doubts about going, for sure. I was definitely in over my head and at times wanted out, but the people at the mosque were excited for me, and Aadam had told all of his friends that I was coming. His family was excited about me coming there to live with them as well. I was feeling a lot of pressure, and there were nights I lay in bed, thinking about my parents crying and being devastated that I'd left. I knew what I was doing was a terrible thing to do to them, but the plan was too far along to stop. It really killed me to see what I was doing to my parents.

In my heart, I knew that everything I'd been preparing for was right in front of me. This was my ticket to see Aadam, the man I loved and had sacrificed everything for. I took a deep breath and hit confirm. I sat there for a second in some sort of shock. I turned to

> I sat there for a couple of minutes with my mouse hovering over the "confirm purchase" button. *Was this really what I wanted to do?*

Hadiya, and she gave me a hug. It was reassurance that what I was doing was the right thing, but I'll admit I still felt queasy and nervous about what I'd done. I drank some water and decided to head home.

The next day, I received an email from the airline, which informed me that my purchase wasn't authorized because there was a $500 daily limit on my bank account. I had the same feeling I felt when I discovered my passport was missing; I was anxious and panicked. I went online to see if airline tickets to Kosovo were still the same price. Fortunately, they hadn't increased yet. After school that day, I went to the bank and opened a "college checking account," which had a $2,000 daily limit, and moved my money to that account. Even better: my mom wouldn't have access to the account and couldn't track what I was buying.

My departure date was only five days away, but I decided I wouldn't immediately buy an airline ticket. I'd do it later that night or even the next day. I wasn't looking forward to feeling the guilt about clicking "confirm purchase" again. Honestly, that button represented so much more than purchasing a plane ticket. I was "confirming" leaving my family, my friends, my life, and my faith. I was going to walk away from everyone who cared about me, and I was confirming flipping my family's life upside down.

I can't lie: As the big day approached, I felt a whirlwind of emotions. It was exhilarating to think about my future with Aadam, but it was also incredibly draining. I couldn't stop thinking about how amazing it was going to be with him, but I couldn't get my family off my mind. I knew that within days I was going to shatter their world. Every time I looked at my family, I wanted to cry. It even got to the point where I couldn't make eye contact with my parents and brothers because I knew I would be overwhelmed by emotions.

As my time with my family wound down, I often thought about the little things I would miss about my parents. My dad gave the best hugs. He is a very large man, and his hand can grasp a basketball. I thought about how much my dad and I had done together. He'd worked so hard to have a relationship with me built on trust and love. I would miss how he cooked every meal and even the punch lines of his corny jokes. When I looked at my mom, I'd realize how much I was going to miss our late-night conversations and watching TV shows together. We often went on walks together at night to talk about the past week's events. We hadn't taken one of those walks in about a year, and I was beginning to realize that they'd never happen again. Even if I did return to the United States one day, I knew things would be different between my family and me.

To this day, I've never felt as much sympathy for someone else as I did in those moments. I felt guilty about what I was doing. I knew my brothers didn't know anything about what was going on, but they were going to wake up one day and not have a sister anymore. I also thought about how my parents would never see my wedding, which I was sure was something they'd always looked forward to.

I tried not to think about the things I'd miss and they'd miss, but sometimes the thoughts would still creep into my head. I'd break down for a few minutes in private, but then I'd dry my eyes and act as if I didn't have any feelings at all. It was easier that way.

Eventually I started to tell myself that it was a good thing that I was leaving home, that my parents and I needed time apart from each other. But in my heart, I knew that I was only trying to justify what I was doing. It's amazing what the human mind can do in order to suppress your true feelings. I knew how my parents and brothers would feel about me leaving, but I lied to myself, saying they would be okay and would actually want me out of the house because I was Muslim. I was now a bad influence on my brothers, I told myself, and it would be a good thing if I weren't around to corrupt them.

I still dreaded the phone call I'd have to make to my parents from New York, before I boarded a plane to Switzerland and then Kosovo, when I would finally tell them where I was going and that I didn't know when I was coming back. In those final days, I did think about calling the entire thing off and staying in the United States, but only very briefly and in my weakest moments.

While part of me was breaking down because of what I was about to do to my family, I could barely temper my excitement about where I was going. In less than a week, I would see Aadam and be with him after waiting so long. Finally, our long conversations and detailed plans were coming to fruition. I kept imagining the moment when I'd get off the plane and see him standing there. I thought about how amazing it was going to feel to run to him and jump into his arms like I'd seen other couples do in the movies. I felt that once I was with him, my life would finally be in order. The strain, heartache, and pressure of the past year would finally be worth it once I got off that plane.

CHAPTER 20

Moment of Truth

John

It was the morning of Wednesday, June 4, and I'd just hung up the phone with Agent Sheridan, who informed me that he and two other FBI agents were en route to our house and would arrive in about twenty minutes. Stephanie and I drew a breath and stepped into the living room, where her mother and father were watching TV. While awaiting back surgery, her father was taking heavy medication and was often weak and confused. Thankfully, that morning he was alert and attentive. Stephanie asked for their attention and then told them that we didn't have time to explain, but three FBI agents were headed to our house. She told them that they needed to know that Mackenzie was in a lot of trouble, and we wanted them to go into the bedroom and remain there until we told them it was okay to come out. As to be expected, Stephanie's mom immediately started asking us a series of questions. Thankfully, my father-in-law interrupted her and said with surprising

153

resolve and clarity, "Honey, let's do as they ask." She looked at him, then us, and nodded. They went to the bedroom and closed the door.

At about ten o'clock in the morning, three dark sedans turned the corner and parked in quick succession in front of our house. A man wearing a dark suit promptly emerged from each one. If any of our neighbors noticed, I'm sure it looked like a scene from a TV police drama. I answered the door before the agents even knocked.

Three dark sedans parked in front of our house. A man wearing a dark suit promptly emerged from each one.

Agent Sheridan introduced me to his colleagues, including Special Agent El-Sayed, the Muslim FBI agent he had told us about. Agent Sheridan quickly got down to business and instructed Stephanie to pick up Mackenzie from Plano West Senior High School. He told her to tell Mack that there was an emergency at home, that the FBI wanted to talk to her, and that she needed to come home immediately. He also instructed Stephanie not to answer any of Mackenzie's questions or let her use her phone. He told Stephanie to enter our house through the front door when they returned. Before Stephanie left, Agent Sheridan warned us that it was going to be a difficult meeting, and that it was important we act like we'd never heard any of the details about what was being discussed. Before Stephanie left to pick up Mack, she and I had a single prayer: "Jesus, please let this work."

As Stephanie pulled away, the agents discussed among themselves how they wanted to conduct the interview, and worked out the fine details. They decided whether to keep their coats on or off, whether to stack our family passports so they could be seen or hidden from view until needed, and even where each individual would sit around the table. I watched and listened silently, while quietly considering how grateful I was to have this kind of help.

Stephanie told me later that she'd found Mack's car in the parking lot at the high school and waited several minutes for her to return from taking final exams. Her mind had raced as she thought about what to do and say. Keeping Mack from using her cell phone was paramount, and she'd decided that the best thing to do was have Mack drive her Mazda Tribute, which had a manual transmission. Finally, Mackenzie approached the car and stared blankly when she saw her mother standing there. "What are you doing here?" she asked.

"The FBI is at the house and wants to talk to you," Stephanie told her.

"Why?" Mackenzie asked her.

"I have no clue," Stephanie answered. "You're eighteen and they won't talk to me!

"You drive," Stephanie said as she opened the passenger door to Mackenzie's car. As they drove home, Mack asked a few questions along the way, mostly different variations of, "What do they want?"

I watched through the front window as the white Tribute pulled up in front of the house. Mackenzie quickly climbed out of the driver's seat with the familiar brown leather messenger bag on her shoulder. In an obvious state of urgency, she marched up the sidewalk with Stephanie right behind her. When Mack entered the house, she immediately saw me sitting at the dining table with three FBI agents. Her familiar teenage scowl dropped. I don't know what she was expecting to see, but this wasn't it. The three agents stood in unison to greet her. As planned, Mackenzie took a seat directly across from Agent Sheridan, with Agent El-Sayed across the table and to her left. The third agent was seated at the head of the table, immediately to her right. Stephanie sat next to Mackenzie, and I was at the opposite end of the table.

Agent Sheridan introduced himself and the other FBI agents to Mackenzie, and with a show of formality, they slid their credentials and business cards in front of her. Mackenzie was quiet and nervous. Sheridan took immediate control of the meeting and explained they were there because during the course of an investigation her name had come up a few times and they wanted to talk to her about it. He told her the FBI had credible information that she was in contact with a Muslim man who lived in Albania or Kosovo, and that she had even had social media interaction with him. He looked directly at Mackenzie while talking to her, and in a slightly hardened tone warned her that it was important that she was truthful about everything she said to them. Sheridan explained that he and the other agents were going to ask her a lot of questions, some of which they already knew the answers to. He warned her that lying to a federal agent was a criminal offense, punishable by up to five years in prison.

> He warned her that lying to a federal agent was a criminal offense, punishable by up to five years in prison.

One of the other agents then pulled out a form and slid it across the table to Mackenzie. Sheridan explained that it was a Miranda warning, which the FBI fills out when it arrests someone, puts them in handcuffs, and takes them to jail. He reminded Mack that even though she was still in high school, she was also eighteen and no longer a minor. She was subject to federal law as an adult, so it was very important that she tell them the truth. It was obvious that he had Mackenzie's full attention. She acknowledged the warning and promised she would be honest.

"Are you in contact with anyone overseas using social media or a phone? Perhaps someone in Albania or Kosovo?" Sheridan asked her.

"Yes," Mackenzie answered. "His name is Aadam, and he lives in Kosovo. I have been talking to him."

"Why were you talking to him?" Sheridan asked.

Mackenzie told him that she'd met him online and had been talking to him for a while, mostly over the phone or via video chats.

"How long have you been talking to him?" Sheridan continued.

Mackenzie said she'd been talking to Aadam for about a year, since the previous April. Then Sheridan asked what Mackenzie had been talking to him about. Before answering the question, Mack glanced at Stephanie and me. She told Sheridan that she had some questions about Islam, and that Aadam looked nice, so she approached him about her interest in the religion.

"What is the nature of your relationship?" Sheridan asked her.

Mackenzie became visibly nervous and paused before answering. "We're good friends," she said.

Sheridan then shifted gears and reached to his right for a small stack of navy-blue U.S. passports while keeping his eyes locked on Mackenzie. "Let's talk about passports," he said. Clearly uneasy about where the interview was about to go, Mackenzie nodded to him. I watched my daughter closely because I knew we were about to reach the moment of truth.

"I have five passports here, Mackenzie, one for each member of the family, including one for you," Sheridan said. "Do you know where these are kept?"

"Mom keeps them in a safe-deposit box," she answered.

"Mackenzie, is this all of them?" Sheridan asked.

For the first time, I noticed tears forming in Mackenzie's eyes.

"No, I have another one," she admitted.

"Do you know where it is?" Sheridan asked her.

"It's right here," she said. Then Mackenzie reached into her messenger bag and pulled out the duplicate passport. I feigned surprise, but obviously I wasn't.

"Did you apply for a replacement in person or online?" Sheridan asked her in a stern voice.

"Online," she said.

"What reason did you give for needing a new one?"

"I told them I lost the first one."

"But you knew where your first one was?"

"Yes, I did."

Agent Sheridan slowly pulled out a sheet of paper with U.S. Department of State letterhead and pushed it in front of my daughter.

"Mackenzie, I'm glad you answered that question honestly," he said. "Is that your signature?"

"Yes," she admitted.

The gravity of the situation was apparently beginning to dawn on her.

"Mackenzie, you have knowingly secured a U.S. passport fraudulently," Sheridan said. "Passports are proof of U.S. citizenship and are very valuable. Lying in order to get one is a felony. It is punishable by up to five years in prison. So why did you need a passport so badly that you lied to get one?"

With that question, my daughter no longer looked eighteen. She looked small, weak, and afraid. She asked if she had to answer the question in front of us. Sheridan told her that she did not, but added that he thought it would be a good idea if she did. Then the other shoe fell and the truth was finally revealed. Looking at Stephanie and then me, with tears streaming down her face, Mackenzie told us in a soft, broken voice that she was sorry we were finding out this way, and that she never wanted us to find out like this. She turned back to Sheridan and said, "We're engaged. I got it so I could go see him." She turned to us and mouthed, "I'm so sorry," but her voice was only a high whisper.

Agent Sheridan then asked how she was planning to go to Kosovo to see Aadam. Crying openly now, Mackenzie told him that she planned to buy an airline ticket and a friend was going to drive her to the airport. She told him that she'd planned to call us during a layover in New York to tell us good-bye. The words cut through me like a hot knife. It was true. Deep down inside, I had been hoping that maybe it wasn't, but hearing her say it was jarring. She was really going to do it.

> Deep down inside, I had been hoping that maybe it wasn't, but hearing her say it was jarring. She was really going to do it.

After that admission, the hidden facts of her deception unfolded like a bad dream. She told us she was engaged to Aadam under Islamic law and was planning to travel to Kosovo to marry him. She confessed to how she'd converted to Islam months ago and had been attending a mosque in Plano. She said people at the mosque had been helping her for weeks, and they'd even advised her about how to obtain a replacement passport. People at the mosque had assigned her a mentor to show her how to be a "good Muslim wife," and she'd been spending a lot of time with a Muslim family. The agents continued to probe her, asking more detailed questions about Aadam and what role the mosque played in her plan.

Sheridan then asked Mackenzie if she'd received any letters from Aadam. She reached into her messenger bag and pulled out a handwritten letter he'd sent to her. Mack and Sheridan discussed the letter at length, including Aadam's choice of words, his handwriting style, and other nuances and evidence that suggested he was not a typical, uneducated Muslim man from Kosovo. The agents had great insight into the letter because, unbeknownst to Mack, we'd provided them with a copy of it at our first meeting.

During the second hour of the FBI's interview of Mack, she revealed that Aadam hadn't asked her for money and hadn't talked about harming anyone in the United States or abroad. She said he frequently talked about Islam and the mistreatment of Muslims. He hadn't introduced her to anyone in the United States, and she'd only talked to him on the phone and through social media. Hearing her say it herself was like hearing it for the first time. I couldn't believe that despite never meeting him in person, she was prepared to abandon her family, her Christian heritage, and everyone she knew to move to a country she hadn't even known existed until a year ago. Her plan was to become a Muslim housewife living in Kosovo, and she wasn't going to tell us until shortly before she boarded a plane in New York. Tears flowed down Mackenzie's face the entire time, and there was a massive lump in my throat. Stephanie and I remained stoic as the verbal punches rained down on us.

Evidently satisfied that ISIS, al-Qaeda, or some other Islamic extremist group wasn't radicalizing her, Sheridan softened his tone as he started to focus on his concern for her personal safety.

"We are here for two things," he told her. "First to protect the interests of the United States. Secondly, we want to protect the citizens of the United States."

The agents, each of whom had spent more than twenty years working in Islamic countries, explained what life would be like for her if she was, in fact, leaving for a legitimate engagement in Kosovo. They described the severe poverty in the country, as well as the types of fraud that were prevalent there. One of the agents explained that Serbian countries were notorious for instigating marriage fraud for the purpose of embezzling money from someone or obtaining U.S.

citizenship. He told Mack that U.S. citizenship was highly valued in a poor country like Kosovo, and the people there would go to great lengths to obtain it. The agent told her that it could be even more serious if human trafficking or sex trafficking was involved, especially for an attractive eighteen-year-old American girl. The agents didn't hold back any punches, even telling Mack what she'd be worth as a sex slave and what her organs might bring on the black market. The details were grueling, but it was exactly what she needed to hear.

If Mack left for Kosovo, the agents told her, there would be no U.S. protections, and she'd be at the mercy of her captors there. In that part of the world, they explained, it happened all the time. "We bring girls like you home in a body bag every day," one of the agents said. "We want to save you. If you go there, there's a good chance you'll be dead in a week."

El-Sayed, the Muslim agent, also explained to Mackenzie that her engagement probably wasn't even legitimate. He said that very few Muslim families would ever allow a Muslim man to marry a woman who had so recently converted. He said it typically took years for such an arrangement to happen, to ensure that the bride's conversion was legitimate. He said the bride's father and groom's father often arranged a marriage, and Aadam's parents hadn't even contacted us. He said that nothing about her engagement made sense, and it was not the way of Islam. After talking with Mackenzie for a few minutes, Agent El-Sayed asked us if he could speak to her alone. It was a totally unscripted request, but we felt like we didn't have a choice, so we moved to the kitchen. We found out later that he advised Mack to study her Christian faith before deciding to convert to Islam. He told her to first fully understand what she was trying to leave, and to slow down. He told her she was being reckless, and that this was not the way a real Islamic marriage should work. After about fifteen minutes, Stephanie and I returned to the table.

By now the initial shock and confusion were clearing from Mackenzie's head. She started to ask the FBI agents what they knew about Aadam personally. She wondered if they knew for a fact that he was involved in these types of crimes. She asked for evidence that he was, indeed, going to try to hurt her. Agent Sheridan told her that he and the other agents weren't going to answer questions about an ongoing investigation, but they were convinced that she'd be seriously hurt or killed if she went to Kosovo.

"Organized crime is rampant in that part of the world," Sheridan told her. "You have put yourself in extreme danger, and you are fortunate we talked to you before you made a fatal mistake."

After nearly three hours, the meeting was finally coming to an end. The FBI agents were compassionate, professional, and thorough; and Stephanie and I would never be able to thank them enough for their assistance. One of the last things they told Mackenzie was that she should end her relationship with Aadam immediately. Not only was she interfering with their investigation, but she was also putting herself in grave danger. She needed to remove herself from the situation and never contact him again.

Before the agents left our house, El-Sayed offered to answer any questions that Mackenzie might have about Islam in the future, and told her that he was only a telephone call away. Sheridan promised Mackenzie that her health and security were their biggest concerns.

"You were very close to putting yourself into an extremely dangerous situation, and we're just glad we were able to help you," he said. "You've already committed a felony and came very close to getting yourself killed. You need to talk to your parents, and be happy that you have an opportunity to build yourself a bright future here. Mostly, count yourself lucky we were able to stop you before it was too late."

Sheridan told us he'd let us know whether or not the FBI decided to pursue criminal charges against Mackenzie for passport fraud, which we knew wasn't a real possibility. We walked the agents to our door, shook their hands, and thanked them for their help. As I shook Agent Sheridan's hand, he quietly passed me the duplicate passport Mackenzie had surrendered to him a couple of hours earlier for safe-keeping. I knew he was going to do this, since there was no criminal case open, and he had no official grounds to keep it.

When we closed the door, Stephanie, Mackenzie, and I hugged for a short time. We told Mack how much we loved her, but I noticed that something wasn't right. Her hug wasn't as warm or affectionate as it should have been after what had just occurred. I sensed she was no longer upset and concerned; she was now angry about what had happened. She broke from our hug and ran upstairs.

> She was no longer upset and concerned; she was now angry about what had happened. She broke from our hug and ran upstairs.

I followed her upstairs and when I reached her bedroom, I heard her voice through the door. She was screaming at someone: "They knew all about me leaving and the passport. It was the FBI! What have you done? What kind of trouble are you in?"

My heart sank as I listened. The FBI agents were literally still standing in our front yard, and she had ignored their most dire warning and contacted Aadam again. Our intervention hadn't worked, and our second battle with Mackenzie was about to begin. I feared breaking her wish to be with him was going to be more difficult than we had ever imagined.

CHAPTER 21

Denial

John

Mackenzie's cloak of secrecy was now gone, and I was mad. After I abruptly pushed open her bedroom door, I found her sitting on the floor at the foot of her bed with a cell phone pressed to her ear.

"Are you out of your mind?" I asked her forcefully.

"I had to find out if what the FBI said was true," she answered. "They didn't say Aadam had done anything wrong. I had to talk to him and find out."

"Hang up that phone, right now!" I demanded. "You just had three FBI agents here, and with everything you just heard and everything they told you to do, this is your reaction? What are you thinking?"

"I have to talk to him to find out for myself, Dad," Mackenzie argued.

"I don't care! Hang up the phone now!"

"Dad, he said he doesn't know anything about it. He said it is a mistake. He wants to talk to you."

At that point, I'd had enough. I wasn't going to argue with her any longer. "Hang it up!" I insisted.

"He wants to talk to you, Dad!"

"I have no interest in talking to him. Absolutely none. And you shouldn't either. Hang up . . . right now!"

"I've got to go," Mackenzie said into the phone, and she finally ended the call.

"The FBI doesn't just show up at someone's house for no reason, Mackenzie. All the lies you've been telling us! You committed a felony with that passport!" I tried to explain to her. "They told you the danger you are in. They told you to break contact with whoever this is immediately, and despite all that, this is what you do?"

"They didn't say he did anything," she insisted. "If they had something on Aadam, they would have told me, and they didn't do that."

"Mackenzie, they told you not to call him and you did anyway. Not only are you putting yourself in danger, you are putting our whole family in danger."

> "Not only are you putting yourself in danger, you are putting our whole family in danger."

No matter how hard I tried to dissuade her, Mackenzie insisted that Aadam, a man she only knew by what he had shown her online, wasn't involved in the horrible crimes the FBI agents had described to her. She wouldn't consider the possibility that he might put her in harm's way.

"He was totally shocked, Dad," she told me. "He said he hasn't done anything. He has no idea why the FBI would be doing this. He wants to explain it to you."

"There is no way I'm going to talk to him—none! And you shouldn't be talking to him either. Those guys told you plain and simple—do not contact him. That should be enough, but apparently it is not. We're not finished talking about this, Mackenzie. Do not call him back!"

And with that, I shut her bedroom door and walked back downstairs to find Stephanie. Of course, she was aghast when I recounted the events to her. "She has a lot of explaining to do," I told Stephanie. "I really thought this would work, but it doesn't look like it did."

Stephanie reminded me that the most important thing to come out of the intervention was that Mackenzie's plan was now out in the open and she wasn't going anywhere, at least not anywhere outside of the United States, because she no longer had a passport. We had stopped her from leaving, and three weeks earlier I wouldn't have bet you a dollar that we would accomplish that. We had to be thankful that we'd prevented her from jumping on a plane into harm's way. We'd hoped the shock and awe of the FBI intervention would eliminate her desire to leave and scare her enough that she'd end her communication and relationship with Aadam once and for all. Accomplishing our most important goal wasn't bad, but we were still far from finished.

Agent Sheridan called me about an hour later to find out what had transpired after they'd left. Much to my surprise, his reaction was pretty calm when I informed him I'd discovered Mackenzie on her phone with Aadam immediately after they left our house. "Wow, that's a shock," he said. "I don't think we've ever done anything like this and it didn't scare the crap out of the person. For her to call him that quickly is a real surprise." Agent Sheridan said he wanted to talk to Agent El-Sayed about the situation and then he'd be in touch.

Within an hour or two after talking with Agent Sheridan, I opened my laptop and discovered a Facebook Messenger icon indicating an incoming message. When I opened it, I was surprised to see it was from Aadam, directly to my account. I assumed he was able to get my Facebook information from Mackenzie's account. The message was written in very broken English and read in part:

Hi Sir . . please I just wanted to tell u that I love you all becose I love Mackenzie im just a simple student that met a really good girl and im in love with her and I just wanted to come there and live with u all that is a mistake what I heard FBI thing nothing its true I swear in God about my parents they are so happy about us they are simply parents that wants happiness about their Son they even were sad about Mackenzie not telling u anything cuz they wanted to tell you everything . . . please I just Love Her that's all I will go to the US embassy here and they went they just told me what to do please its all a mistake im honest I just started loving Mike and Luike they are so cute plaz help us.

About an hour later, I received another Facebook message from him:

Answer me Sir plz I know you are really good person She told me a lot about uu This is all mistake someone from jealous could do this because we are so happy with each other I really didn't want her to hide this by you but she was just scared then we waited to skype you later I will do anything what you want but please don't break up us im scared for her she will be so sad and I want to make her happy. ☹

ims justa sincere person I want to love to live in happiness. Im studying economy and im in the last year then I was planning with Mackenzie to study together there but me in master I swear this is the true im;s ready to declear anything what fbi said. I started loving u all: (I even said to Mack that can I call u Dad cuz I needed a family when I come there☹.

Then another message came about an hour later:

I'm so scared sir☹((why this happened we were so happy and good. A lot of foreign girls comes here I haven't seen any problem never.

My first instinct was to respond back and spell out exactly how I felt about this whole situation he had created. But, understanding that a level head was needed, I sent the messages from Aadam to Agent Sheridan and asked his opinion on whether or not I should respond. Within minutes Sheridan called me. We discussed the messages at length, and at first we were leaning toward me responding, but the more we discussed it, the more I became convinced it would be a mistake. What good could possibly come out of me making contact with him? I decided I wouldn't respond in any way, nor would I make any type of contact with him in any form or fashion. Agent Sheridan and Stephanie agreed with my decision.

im just a simple student that met a really good girl and im in love with her and I just wanted to come there and live with u all.

When Stephanie and I first devised the plan to confront Mackenzie about her deception, we'd hoped that she would run back to her family for safety and protection. Instead, after the very tenuous meeting with the FBI, we were met with defiance, anger, and arrogance. Now Stephanie and I had an important decision to make: Should we shut down everything—phone, money, and car? I consulted with Agent Sheridan, and he advised us not to do it.

He correctly pointed out that Mack didn't have the capacity to go anywhere without a passport, and the security holds he'd requested were still in place at Dallas/Fort Worth International Airport and the other international airports. What Agent Sheridan said made sense, and Stephanie and I decided not to drop the hammer on Mack immediately. Of course, we still had the option of going there in the future if needed.

That night, Mackenzie said she wanted to talk to her friend Jordyn and asked if she could go to her house. We agreed to let her go, and as soon as she left the house, I turned on the GPS tracker. Instead of heading south on the tollway toward Jordyn's house, she turned north and drove to the mosque. I called Sheridan and we came up with another plan. When Mackenzie returned home later that night, Stephanie asked her how her visit with Jordyn went. Mackenzie looked her straight in the eye and said Jordyn was doing fine, and even provided details of her visit. She'd lied to us, but we no longer had to worry about secrecy. I confronted her and told her we'd just spoken to the FBI, and we knew she'd been to the mosque.

"What?" she asked. "They have people following me now?"

"They sat here right at that table and told you to separate yourself from all of this immediately, and you're not doing it!" I told her.

"I don't understand!" she continued. "Am I being followed? What is happening?"

"I only know what they told you to do," I said. "And I know that you just lied to us again. How are we supposed to know what is the truth with you anymore? You feel like you can just tell us whatever you want, and lie about anything you don't want us to know about."

And with that condemnation, Mackenzie went upstairs. The long day had finally ended, and things were a lot different now. She now realized it would be much more difficult to hide her secrets, and when things are in the light, they're harder to hide.

Stephanie and I had no idea what to do next. Yes, the threat of Mackenzie leaving the country was gone, so changing her mind and eliminating her desire to leave were our priorities. But we needed to focus on Aadam as well and find out as much as we could about him so we could prove to Mack that he wasn't who she believed he was. We also had to figure out what the people at the mosque were telling her and what role they might have played in trying to help her travel to Kosovo. Fortunately, we still had the help of the FBI in finding those answers.

During our intervention, Agent El-Sayed had graciously offered to talk to Mackenzie about Islam at any time, and she called him the very next day. It was the first of many conversations they would have during the next few weeks. During their initial phone call, he advised her that she needed to figure out whether the man in Kosovo was genuine or not. He pointed out that Aadam didn't have a job, and he couldn't understand why not. Aadam could speak somewhat fluent English, which was a valuable skill in that part of the world, and yet he still wasn't working. That was a significant red flag, according to Agent El-Sayed. He once again encouraged Mackenzie to slow down, telling her she didn't know enough about Islam or Aadam to do something so drastic.

Agent El-Sayed also encouraged Mackenzie to learn more about Islam, and he advised her to first learn the Bible and then compare it to the Koran before she made a definitive decision about her faith. He pointed out that the Koran, like the Bible, teaches us that we're supposed to respect our parents, and that started with her not lying to us anymore. Finally, Agent El-Sayed revealed to Mack that he'd been in contact with the president of the mosque she was attending, and had advised him to change the mentor who was assigned to Mackenzie because the woman was giving her bad and reckless advice. Agent El-Sayed also discovered that the mosque had offered to pay to bring Aadam to the United States on a non-working visa. El-Sayed asked the mosque president to withdraw the offer immediately, which he did.

At the end of their conversation, Mackenzie admitted to Agent El-Sayed that she was thankful for the intervention, but still wasn't convinced that Aadam was trying to hurt her. He gave her strict instructions not to plan to marry Aadam without proof that he was legitimate. I have to admit I wasn't thrilled about Agent El-Sayed keeping open the doors to religious conversion and marriage, but he also viewed things differently from me. And, actually, he provided her with pretty sound advice, and we were happy that she was at least talking and listening to someone other than Aadam.

> I wasn't thrilled about Agent El-Sayed keeping open the doors to religious conversion and marriage, but he actually provided her with pretty sound advice.

By the end of the week, Mackenzie had dramatically shifted gears. She no longer wanted to travel to Kosovo to marry Aadam; she now wanted to bring her "fiancé" to America instead. Fortunately, Agent El-Sayed had persuaded the mosque not to finance his trip here. Mackenzie still wanted me to talk to Aadam, but that simply wasn't going to happen. However, her continued desire to be with him didn't dilute our happiness and relief about stopping her from leaving. She wasn't nearly as upset as we thought she'd be about having to stay; in fact, she never once said, "I wish you had not stopped me."

But now we had to find a way to reconnect with our daughter and rebuild our relationship. Bringing her back into our family wasn't going to be easy, because she'd been emotionally separated from us for so long.

CHAPTER 22

Fighting for Her Heart and Soul

John

On Saturday, June 7, which was the day Mackenzie was supposed to leave for Kosovo, I thought I would try to take her back to one of her first loves—horses. She and I made a trip to Lone Star Park, a Thoroughbred-racing venue in Grand Prairie, Texas. No horse is as beautiful as a Thoroughbred, and I thought watching the races would be a great way for us to spend some quality time together and talk about something other than the FBI, Kosovo, and Islam.

For the most part, it was a wonderful evening. We chatted about regular things, admired the horses, and even laughed together a little bit. We did spend some time talking about Aadam and her desire for him to come to the United States. I didn't make much progress in changing her mind about Islam or being with him, but our discussions were not heated. Throughout the night, I found myself looking at her and thinking about how different the evening would have been if we had not been able to intervene and stop her.

Since the intervention three days earlier, our conversations with Mackenzie had been markedly different. While Stephanie and I were plotting to stop her from leaving, we were very cautious not to create tension of any kind, which might have caused her to leave immediately. Now that everything was in the open, we were having brutally honest discussions with her; they were controlled and respectful, but intense.

> Now that everything was in the open, we were having brutally honest discussions with Mackenzie; they were controlled and respectful, but intense.

In the past, we'd argued with her almost exclusively about theology. Now that we understood the root of her Islamic conversion, things were much clearer for us. Mackenzie was adamant she was now a Muslim, whether we liked it or not, and she was engaged to marry Aadam. Stephanie and I didn't even try to address her Muslim conversion; we'd been banging our heads against that wall for more than a year and had made zero progress.

But we hit her engagement directly and hard, and questioned how she could possibly marry someone she had never met face-to-face. What kind of engagement was that? Agent El-Sayed had already told her that the arrangement was contrary to many Islamic religious and cultural traditions. Additionally, why would she want to place herself in a lifestyle she knew did not suit her? We continued to point out the differences in status of women in the mosque itself and the cultural expectation of Muslim women bearing the load of housework and raising children. Of course, we were once again met with a barrage of circular reasoning that eventually seemed to always end up with, "You are not Muslim, so you don't understand."

Mackenzie was focused on how to get Aadam to the United

States, and she took a hardened stance when I asked her how his family was going to pay for the airfare, as well as how he'd pay for living expenses here if he didn't have a job. One of the more interesting things we observed was that we never saw her cry or express sadness that she might not be able to be with him. We saw only a strong determination that she was somehow going to make it work.

A couple of hours after Mackenzie and I returned from our enjoyable time at the horse races, the brief honeymoon ended. I went to bed before Stephanie that night, and the next morning Stephanie told me that Mackenzie had approached her and demanded to know when she was going to get her passport back. This obviously alarmed us greatly, because we thought she had given up on wanting to leave the country. All the conversations since the FBI meeting had been about how to get Aadam over here. When Stephanie refused to give her a promise as to when the passport would be returned, Mackenzie said she could call the police if we didn't give it back to her, then insinuated she might travel to Macedonia, where Aadam supposedly had dual citizenship. It was an empty threat spoken out of frustration. We knew, and she knew, she no longer had any way to get another passport. But the incident reminded us that Mack wasn't thinking clearly or logically and that she was listening to someone else—Aadam, somebody at the mosque, or both.

No matter where Stephanie and I turned, we seemed to be constantly fighting against what people at the mosque were telling her. It was clear they'd been involved in our daughter's life for a while. It was also increasingly evident that we needed to partner with someone there to persuade Mackenzie to break it off with Aadam. We figured getting into a religious debate with the mosque would be pointless, but we hoped someone there would partner with us and tell Mack that she needed to end her relationship with a man who might hurt her. And it was important to me that if she indeed ended up traveling overseas, and something terrible happened to her, I needed to know that I'd done everything possible to try to stop her.

I was convinced I needed to have a face-to-face meeting with someone at the mosque. I wanted them to see that we weren't raving maniacs, and that we only wanted our daughter to be safe. On Sunday morning, I sent an email to Agent Sheridan, asking if Agent El-Sayed would help us arrange a meeting with the leadership at the mosque. Agent El-Sayed emailed me back within the hour and informed me that the mosque president was out of town, but the secretary had agreed to meet with us at four o'clock that afternoon. Agent El-Sayed told me he wouldn't be able to make it, so it would only be the mosque secretary, Mackenzie, and us at the meeting.

Around ten, we woke up Mackenzie and told her about the meeting we had just scheduled for that afternoon. She didn't take it well. In fact, we've had Texas tornadoes that weren't as loud.

"That's my family! That's my people!" she screamed. "You have no right being involved in my world!"

Stephanie and I remained calm and told her firmly, "We're sorry you feel that way, but we're going to do this. You're welcome to come with us, or not. It is your choice. But we're going, with you or without you." She was livid.

Agent El-Sayed also sent Mackenzie a text message, which read in part:

Please do not be offended by all of this. We all want to make sure you are safe. I think this meeting will

give your parents the peace of mind that you are
dealing with normal human beings, not a cult.

Later that afternoon, we arrived at the mosque a few minutes
early. Before we went in, I reminded Stephanie that, given the
Muslim culture, it would probably be best if I took the lead in the
meeting, and she concurred. We reminded each other that we
had to stay away from debating religion and focus on Mackenzie's
safety and ending her relationship with Aadam. Mackenzie had
reluctantly agreed to go to the meeting, but she didn't ride to the
mosque with us. When we walked inside, we were told the secretary
wasn't there yet.

Mackenzie wanted to give us a tour of the mosque, and we were
surprised by her familiarity with it. It was clear that she had been
there many times before. She was careful to show us which areas
were considered sacred and told us where we were not allowed to
enter. She showed us the prayer room from a distance and where
women had to pray. It was very difficult to hear how comfortable
she'd become with Islam, but we didn't say anything. It clearly
wasn't the time or place to voice our displeasure. But when Mackenzie left to find the secretary, I stared at a mosaic on the wall and
felt an extreme sense of grief. Standing in that mosque hallway, it hit
me just how far Mack had strayed from her faith and family.

The secretary arrived and greeted us. He was wearing a traditional white Muslim robe, sandals, and a white headdress. He took
a seat at the head of a long table; I sat to his left and Stephanie to his
right. Mackenzie found a seat to my left, with two chairs between us.
The mood in the room was noticeably tense. After brief small talk,
I asked the secretary if he was familiar with my daughter's situation.
He told us the mosque president had briefed him that morning, but
he didn't know many details.

"This meeting has nothing to do with her conversion to Islam," I told the secretary. "We did not agree with it and we did not like it, but she is eighteen years old, and she has to make those decisions for herself. The only thing we are here to discuss is her safety. She is involved in an overseas relationship that we and the FBI are convinced is dangerous, and we want to partner with the mosque to help us convince Mackenzie to break it off immediately."

Then I started at the beginning and explained how Mack and Aadam had met online and had a secret relationship for more than a year that led to their engagement. The situation had only come to light to us in the last few days, I told him; and we'd stopped her from secretly leaving the United States only days before she was supposed to leave. I advised him that we were aware the mosque had arranged for her to have a mentor.

I offered two scenarios to the secretary: the relationship was legitimate, or it was a fraudulent scheme that put my daughter's life in serious danger. Even if Aadam's intentions were legitimate, I argued, there were serious problems: He had no job, no money, and wanted Mackenzie to provide him financial support to come to America. He had no financial means to support himself, let alone a wife and family. On top of that, Mack had only recently converted to Islam and wasn't ready for marriage. If Aadam's intentions were illegitimate, there were obvious risks like human trafficking, sex trafficking, or financial fraud.

> "I need your help, because she will listen to you over us right now."

"I want the mosque leadership to partner with us to tell Mackenzie to break it off with this man immediately," I said. "There are problems in this situation, no matter how you look at it, and her life is in danger. I need your help, because she will listen to you over us right now."

The secretary listened silently, and then spoke to us in a soft and polite voice. He looked at Mackenzie, who had remained quiet, but her disposition was now dark and brooding.

"Do you have a place to worship?" he asked her.

Mackenzie told him that she'd been coming to the mosque, and we hadn't tried to stop her.

"Do you have a place for her to say her prayers at home?" he asked.

We didn't wait for Mackenzie to answer him.

"We allow her to come to the mosque, but we told Mackenzie she is not allowed to practice Islam in our home," I said. "Ours is a Christian home, and we will not allow a non-Christian religion to be practiced there. She has two younger brothers, and we do not want them confused by seeing their sister practice a non-Christian religion."

"Perhaps she could say her prayers in her room, in a way that is not observed by anyone in the house?" he suggested.

"No, she will not be allowed to do that in our home," I insisted.

For the first time, Stephanie joined the conversation.

"Mackenzie said you have teenage children," she said. "Let me ask you this: If one of them came home and said they were converting to Christianity, would you allow them to practice Christianity in your home? Or allow them to practice Christianity in the privacy of their bedroom? Would you allow them to listen to Billy Graham tapes or listen to Christian music or read the Bible?"

The secretary paused and seemed to struggle as to how to respond to Stephanie's question. When he finally spoke, he attempted to deflect the question.

"Sometimes young children need to experience new things, like baseball," he said. "You allow them to try baseball, even if you don't like baseball or don't know how to play, and you let them make their own choice if they want to play the sport or not."

"You didn't answer my question," Stephanie insisted. "Would you allow your child to practice Christianity in your home?"

The secretary continued to talk around her question, but he never gave us a direct answer. Finally, to avoid our discussion from becoming argumentative, I said, "Obviously, this is a much more serious question than a kid playing baseball."

The mosque secretary then switched gears. He looked directly at Mackenzie and said, "Perhaps you could move in with a roommate from the mosque, who could teach you how a Muslim girl lives."

Mackenzie's head shot up at the suggestion, and she responded a bit too loudly, "No, I don't want to do that!"

"Then perhaps you could move in with a Muslim family," the secretary said. "We have families here with girls your age that would allow you to live with them."

Before Mackenzie could reply, seeing the opportunity to make a point, I said, "You know, I think that would be a good idea. We'd be open to that."

Mackenzie shouted again, this time even more angrily, "No! I do not want to do that either!"

The secretary appeared to be genuinely confused by the tone of her response.

"Then what do you want?" he asked her.

"I just want to be with him!"

Stephanie and I let the silence in the room linger for a long moment. The truth had finally been revealed. Her Islamic conversion had little to do with religion; it had everything to do with Aadam.

Angry and frustrated about what had happened, Mackenzie

looked at me and said, "All I want you to do is talk to him, and you will not talk to him."

"I am not going to do that," I told her.

The mosque secretary then explained to Mack that it is customary in the Islamic religion for a bride's father to interview a potential son-in-law and provide a blessing on the marriage. The secretary said his own father had interviewed his sisters' husbands before he allowed them to marry, and on occasion he himself had personally interviewed the suitors to determine whether they were suitable for his sisters or not. Then the conversation took a dramatic turn for the worse. The secretary suggested he would be happy to call Aadam and conduct the interview on my behalf. Stephanie and I nearly jumped out of our chairs when we heard his offer.

"What in the world makes you think you can interview someone to see if he's suitable for Mackenzie when you just met her?" Stephanie asked. "You don't even know her. What basis would you have to make a decision on who was compatible for her?"

When Stephanie was finished, I sat forward on the edge of my seat and leaned over the table. I looked the secretary squarely in the eyes and spoke slowly and forcefully while I emphatically tapped my finger on the table.

"Let me make this perfectly clear," I told him. "I am not delegating my fatherly responsibilities to anyone—not to you, not to the mosque, not to anyone! No one will ever be allowed to speak on my behalf on this matter. There is not to be any misunderstanding on that point."

My words hung in the air for a moment, and the secretary didn't respond. He knew there wouldn't be any further discussion about that matter. I tried to steer the conversation back to our main objective.

"We are here to talk about Mackenzie's safety," I repeated to him.

"Her relationship with this man is putting her at risk. We need the mosque's help in convincing her that this relationship is dangerous and needs to be broken off. I'd rather have a live Muslim daughter than a dead daughter."

The secretary didn't make us any promises. When our meeting ended, he asked to speak to Mackenzie alone. We hoped he would recognize that there was much more to the story and that much of the reason for Mackenzie's conversion stemmed from her relationship with Aadam. We left the mosque slightly discouraged that we didn't get the outright alignment on her safety that we were seeking, but I felt confident that the secretary saw us as caring parents who were more concerned with her safety than blindly lashing out at her conversion. We also felt the meeting was important because Mackenzie had been accustomed to the mosque being a secret place in which she controlled what they knew about her and us. All in all, we felt another barrier had been breached and that things were even more open today than they were before.

When Mackenzie came home later that night, her anger had subsided. We never talked about the meeting again, but Stephanie and I had made our point: we were going to go wherever and talk to whoever we had to, in order to keep her safe. The fight for Mack's heart and soul continued.

CHAPTER 23

Coming Storm

John

It has often been said that a family's love is life's greatest blessing, and that's never truer than during a crisis or tragedy. Stephanie leaned heavily on her sister, Debbie, who offered us prayers, encouragement, and wonderful advice. I'd relied mightily on my family as well, and I called on my mother, brothers, and sisters at different times. My sister Jill provided loving support and encouragement; and my sister Kathy, who had raised a rebellious youth of her own, understood perhaps more than anyone the challenges we were facing. But it was my brother, Paul, who gave me the most practical piece of advice. Paul is not a spiritual person, but he is one of the most observant men I know, especially when it comes to people. He has a deep capacity to empathize with others, which is an attribute most people do not know or truly appreciate about him.

On Sunday night, only four days after the intervention, and a few hours after our meeting at the mosque, I was feeling anxious and called my brother. I could sense a violent storm coming, and I felt it was coming soon. We talked for a long while, as I recapped the dramatic events of the week and the challenges we were still facing with Mackenzie. Finally, I got around to what was bothering me the most. "What am I going to do when she says, 'Either bring him over here, or I'm going over there'?" I asked him.

There was a momentary pause in our conversation, and I thought for a second the line had gone dead, but it hadn't. In a wise and humble way, Paul explained that everything I was describing to him about Mack's behavior and reasoning sounded like someone dealing with an addition to drugs or alcohol. People with addictions do not make rational decisions, he said, and an addict will typically tell you that they know they shouldn't drink or take drugs, they know the dangers of it, and they know the consequences of using them. But they do it anyway because of their addiction. It sounded exactly like Mackenzie's behavior during the past fourteen months. She was rationalizing everything to get what she wanted, even if it made absolutely no logical sense.

"You cannot put rational thoughts in an irrational person, and expect rational actions to come out."

Paul told me that most addicts hit rock bottom, and that's when I would face the question I presented to him about Mackenzie and Aadam.

"John, you cannot put rational thoughts in an irrational person, and expect rational actions to come out," Paul said. "It will always come out irrational. You have to accept that, and if this question comes up, do not leave anything open for interpretation."

Somehow, my brother had reached into the dark room in which I'd been trapped, turned on a light, and explained things for what they were. The behavior he'd described was exactly what Mackenzie was doing, and he'd told me precisely what I needed to hear. I had to stand my ground on what I believed was best—especially when that irrational, rock-bottom moment came for Mackenzie. Just before I was ready to hang up the phone, Paul stopped me.

"John, there's one more thing I want to tell you," he said. "I want to tell you that you also need to rely on your faith. Your faith is really strong and it's something you should rely on. I wish I had that. You have it, and you need to rely on that right now. It will help you."

I will never forget what my brother told me that night. I hung up the phone and looked at Stephanie, who was sitting in my office with me. We both knew Paul was much more pragmatic than spiritual. "You're not going to believe what he just told me," I told Stephanie. "He said I needed to rely on my faith. Can you believe that he told me that?"

It was truly a moment that strengthened me, and it deepened my respect and love for my brother even more.

Two days later, the storm I was anticipating arrived with fury. Mackenzie came into my office on Tuesday night frustrated and irritated. She evidently had been in contact with Aadam again, and she wanted to know why I would not talk to him. She told me he was getting angry that I wouldn't speak to him, and so was she. At the heart of the matter, she wanted me to sponsor Aadam to come to the United States. He couldn't get here any other way, and she wanted me to help pay for his trip so we could meet him. If he could come to Texas for only three or four weeks, we would see how good of a guy he was, that he truly loved her, and that he was only trying to make a better life for himself. On the other hand, if it didn't work out, he would go back to Kosovo.

After patiently listening to Mackenzie's plan, I tried to calmly explain why I didn't think it was a good idea. But my daughter wasn't interested in listening to me. The more I talked to her and explained why I didn't want Aadam to come to the United States, the angrier she became. Nonetheless, I would not budge and hardened my position.

"I will not facilitate something that I do not think is in your best interest," I told her. "And I won't talk to him for the same reason."

"Will you talk to him if he gets over here on his own?" she asked.

"Absolutely not," I replied. "He has been manipulating this situation for a long time. The FBI has warned you to stay away from him, and you are not doing that. I have no intention of talking to him now or ever."

Then the storm came.

Mackenzie's face was flushed with anger and frustration. Looking directly in my eyes, she said, "Dad, then you are forcing me to make a decision. I will be with him someday. So if you do not help him get here like I'm asking you to do, then I will go over there, and you won't be able to stop me. And if something happens to me when I go there, then it's going to be your fault, because you won't help me bring him here. I swear to you I'll do it."

"If something happens to me when I go there, then it's going to be your fault, because you won't help me bring him here. I swear to you I'll do it."

Mackenzie never took her eyes off of me as she defiantly delivered her ultimatum. She was furious, and I knew she was serious. With an even and low voice, I told her, "Mackenzie, you are forcing me to make a choice between two bad decisions. Either I bring him here, which I don't believe is safe for you, or you will go over there on your own, which I also don't believe is safe for you. And that is the choice you're telling me I have to make?"

"Yes," she said.

"You say that if I refuse to help him come here, you'll go over there."

"Yes."

"Then I'm telling you to go buy your plane ticket, because my decision is made, and it is 'no,'" I told her. "I'm not helping bring him here. Not now, not later, and not ever. I will not help him. I will not talk to him, write to him, or acknowledge him. Now you are the one with a choice to make, not me.

"And I will tell you this: If you decide to go over there knowing what you know, knowing what Agent Sheridan and Agent El-Sayed have told you about how dangerous it is over there, and you still decide to go anyway, then you are a fool. And if you decide to go over there and something happens, I will tell you that I can live with myself, because there is absolutely nothing else we could have done to stop you. So now you decide what you want to do. My decision is made."

After turning the tables on Mackenzie, I got up from my chair and walked out of my office without saying another word. She didn't say anything and didn't follow me. After about fifteen minutes, she came into the living room, where Stephanie and I were sitting.

"I don't want to go there, okay?" she admitted. "I just want to bring him here, so we can be sure."

Stephanie and I discussed the situation with Mack once again, but we held firm to our decision and the reasons we believed it was not a good idea to bring Aadam to the United States. Mackenzie had taken her best shot, thrown her best punches, but we were still standing.

There was no apparent end in sight to our standoff with Mackenzie. Progress to convince her to distance herself from Aadam was slowing down and I was worried. The one thing in which I could find solace was that no matter how this worked out, I would be able to look in the mirror and say Stephanie and I had done everything we could to keep her safe. We had played every card we had and it was beginning to look like we were going to fall short. That changed on Friday, June 13, when Agent El-Sayed, who was out of the country on assignment, sent an email to Agent Sheridan and me. The message was an absolute bombshell:

> The secretary from the Plano mosque called me at 2:00 a.m., Middle East time, to discuss MacKenzie. The Secretary advised that after looking at Aadam's Facebook and consulting with a member of the mosque who is from Kosovo, he is very positive that Aadam is using Mackenzie to get to the U.S. and become a citizen. He had a conversation with Mackenzie, and he wants John to call him to discuss some ideas to help Mackenzie forget about Aadam.

Finally, we had something directly from the mosque that at least partially validated our fears. This email showed me that members of the mosque, after a year of supporting this relationship, now knew something was wrong. Agent Sheridan and I were certain the dangers were much higher than a citizenship scam, but it didn't matter. If the mosque leadership told Mackenzie they knew Aadam was deceiving her, it would likely be enough to convince her that the entire thing was a sham and finally break it off with him, ending this nightmare. Now all I had to do was convince the mosque to take that step.

That night, I talked to Mackenzie about her meetings at the mosque, but she gave no indication that anyone there had told her anything about what they'd decided about Aadam. I called the secretary the next day, and after a long conversation, it was clear the mosque had a different idea about what to do than I did. The secretary explained that he'd advised Mackenzie to go to college, let Aadam pay his own way to the United States, and that the mosque was working to get her affiliated with other Muslims to help in her conversion.

Obviously, it wasn't what I wanted to hear. When I asked the secretary why he hadn't yet told Mackenzie about Aadam's scheme, he said he didn't think she was ready to hear that information. In fact, he was probably going to wait three weeks or longer to tell her the news. I explained that wasn't soon enough and asked him to tell her by the next week at the latest. Thankfully, the secretary agreed, but added that he'd have someone else tell her because he didn't want to risk damaging his relationship with Mackenzie.

After my phone call with the mosque secretary, I immediately emailed Agent El-Sayed, copying Agent Sheridan, and asked if I could share his previous email to me with Mackenzie, to show her what the mosque had discovered about Aadam:

> Agent El-Sayed, I feel this information is important to share with her as soon as possible. Would you have strong objections with me sharing your email with her? I want to work with her with facts and not string this out further. We are here, we have counseling lined up to help us, and we have worked hard to ensure our relationship and communication lines with her are open. As we have always stated, we are not standing in the way of her conversion. But we feel it is imperative that she understands the mosque shares our concerns as soon as possible.

Since Agent El-Sayed was out of the country on assignment, Agent Sheridan called me right away and told me to hold off on sharing the email with Mackenzie. I told him I was ready to do it and was willing to clean up the mess later, but he had another plan. He wanted to meet face-to-face with Mackenzie again.

CHAPTER 24

An Angel Leads the Way

John

Stephanie and I realized our help and support from the FBI was ending soon. Agent Sheridan and Agent El-Sayed couldn't have done more to help us: They saved our daughter, and Stephanie and I will be forever grateful. They developed a plan that prevented Mackenzie from leaving the country and heading into harm's way. Agent Sheridan's regular communication with me helped us avoid confrontation and setbacks with Mack, which was already proving to be an important step in restoring our family to some degree of normalcy. Additionally, he encouraged us to find a counselor for Mackenzie to help her navigate through the aftermath of events.

Agent El-Sayed had worked with Mackenzie personally, advising her on Islam and even encouraging her to study the Christian faith more closely before making a decision on her conversion. His invaluable help in talking directly with mosque leaders about Mackenzie's situation cannot be overstated. He opened doors and minds, which would have been impossible for us to do without his help.

Now we were preparing to meet with Agent Sheridan for the last time, and Stephanie and I were still having concerns about Mackenzie's mind-set and what she might be planning. She was still in contact with Aadam and continued to press us for a way to bring him to the United States. There was nothing else the FBI could do to stop her. At the meeting Agent Sheridan would "return" Mackenzie's passport, which would give him one more opportunity to talk to her directly. After that meeting, Stephanie and I would be on our own.

A few days before our meeting with Agent Sheridan, a seemingly unrelated and sad event occurred that changed everything. Sunday evening, Mackenzie noticed that something was off with her beloved cat, Angel, who was lethargic and not acting right. Mack had had Angel, and her littermate, Cleo, since she was ten years old. Angel hated everyone but Mackenzie, and the bond between those two was strong. Mack was the only person Angel would allow to hold her; everyone else in our house was either scratched or scared away by her hissing. It's the reason we joked that if there ever was a cat that was misnamed, it was definitely Angel.

That night, with Angel obviously in distress, Stephanie was nervous about what might happen if the cat died. She was afraid it might be the final straw, which might make Mack break all ties with home and leave for Kosovo. We took the cat to the vet on Monday morning. We were advised that Angel's blood work was fine, and the vet hydrated her and prescribed an antibiotic. We were told to bring the cat back if she wasn't better in a couple of days. After bringing Angel home, however, it became clear that she wasn't getting better and wouldn't make it through the night.

Not wanting to leave Angel alone, Mackenzie lay on a quilt on the utility room tile floor with her cat curled in her arms. Stephanie slept nearby on the couch, knowing Angel would probably not make it to morning. At around four o'clock on Tuesday morning, Stephanie was wakened by Mackenzie's soulful call of "Moooommmmm!" Stephanie hurried over and dropped down next to Mackenzie, embracing her tightly as they leaned down looking at Angel, who was cradled in Mackenzie's arms, softly gasping for breath. Within minutes, Angel quietly passed away. Mackenzie's grief was raw, and Stephanie embraced her, curled tightly in her mother's arms, her shoulders shaking with sobs while she softly stroked her cherished pet's face.

After a couple of minutes, Mackenzie asked, "Can you go get Dad?"

Stephanie hurried upstairs and awakened me with the news. We were back downstairs within seconds, each of us taking a seat on either side of Mackenzie. Together we held her tightly, as Mackenzie's tears fell on the towel swaddling Angel. It was heartbreaking, and it was the first time in over a year Mackenzie had turned to us for love, comfort, and support.

I called Agent Sheridan later that morning and asked if we could postpone our meeting with him, given what had occurred. He respectfully declined my request and said it was the perfect time for him to talk to Mackenzie. He explained that when tragic things happen, most people tend to let their guard down and are more willing to listen. For added emphasis, he reminded me that if this were a criminal case, he would have the authority to order her to be there, but as a father, he said, "You need to bring her in."

> Together we held her tightly; it was the first time in over a year Mackenzie had turned to us for love, comfort, and support.

We buried Angel in our backyard that morning, followed by a brief family ceremony. About an hour later, Mackenzie and I were on our way to the FBI office. She was very quiet during the entire drive.

Mackenzie

I didn't know Angel's death would have such a profound effect on me. It was as if I'd been holding back my emotions for months, and when she died, everything poured out of me at once. I'd been under so much pressure from Aadam and my parents for so long, I finally couldn't take it anymore. I was devastated.

I'd been under so much pressure from Aadam and my parents for so long, I finally couldn't take it anymore. I was devastated.

I wasn't sure why Agent Sheridan wanted to talk to me again. When my dad and I arrived at his office, he greeted us and led us to a small conference table. The first thing Agent Sheridan told me was that he was going to give me back my passport, which was quite a surprise. Then he told me the FBI wasn't going to criminally charge me for fraudulently obtaining a replacement passport, which was a big weight lifted. Agent Sheridan said he was glad I was safe, and he continued to explain the risks of my communication with Aadam and the potential of bringing him to America. He told me about the history of turmoil in Kosovo, including multiple wars, the presence of organized crime, human trafficking, sex trafficking, and other crimes. He shared gruesome details of crimes in Kosovo, including girls who were killed by getting too close to the criminal element in the Balkan region. My father and I listened as Agent Sheridan told us horrible stories about women just like me.

"They will ask you to pay to bring their other family members to America," Agent Sheridan told me.

"But I can only do so much until I am out of money," I replied.

"No, that's when they go to where the money is," Agent Sheridan continued. "And with you, where does the money trail lead? Right there."

Agent Sheridan pointed at my dad, who was listening intently. I started to get a sinking feeling that he was right.

"How much do you think your dad would pay to save your life?" Agent Sheridan asked me. "Fifty thousand dollars? One hundred thousand dollars? Two hundred and fifty thousand dollars? You see, Mackenzie, you are putting your whole family at risk."

I understood what Agent Sheridan was telling me, but I still wasn't convinced the FBI was certain that Aadam was a criminal. "But are you sure he is like that?" I asked.

Sheridan nodded his head and said firmly, "Yes, I am. If he's not in it directly, he is very close to it, and I'm very sure you are putting yourself and your family in danger."

I was shocked at what Agent Sheridan told me next. He explained that the mosque leadership had conducted its own inquiry and did not like what they'd learned about Aadam. Agent Sheridan advised me to stop my communication with Aadam immediately, and he predicted that once I texted him and told him that he'd have to find his own way to America, he would text me back and ask me to come to Kosovo, marry him, and then we'd come back to the United States in a few months.

"He either wants citizenship or to get you over there for something worse," Agent Sheridan said. "If he were legitimate, he would do what it takes to get here, regardless of how long it takes him. But that is not what this is about."

My mind was numb as I absorbed what Agent Sheridan was telling me. I honestly couldn't comprehend what I was hearing. After an hour, we ended our meeting. Before I left the office, Agent Sheridan encouraged me to look forward. He said I had a bright future, and parents and a family who loved me.

"Figure out what you want to do with your life and make that your focus," he told me. "Step away from all this and move forward to something better."

Then Agent Sheridan reached into his pocket and handed me a red, white, and blue FBI coin.

"I want you to have this as a reminder of what you've been through and how fortunate you are to be alive and well," he said. "I hope you have a wonderful and happy life, and be grateful you have a dad and a mom who love you so much."

As we drove home, I remained quiet and didn't say much to my dad. I was thinking about what I needed to do about Aadam. What if the information Agent Sheridan told me was true? What if Aadam was only using me to get to the United States? What if he was planning to hurt or kill me if I went there? Was everything he'd told me during the previous year nothing but lies?

When we got home, I sat in our study talking to my dad about the meeting. Finally, I decided to text Aadam and tell him that I couldn't help him and that he'd have to get to the United States on his own. He replied to me immediately, saying, "Then you need to come to Kosovo. We can get married over here, then we can go back to America in a few weeks."

As I read the response to my dad, I realized it was exactly what Agent Sheridan had predicted, and reality began to sink in. *Oh, my God! How could this happen?* I thought. I continued texting Aadam, challenging his responses, and it wasn't long before I realized that everything I'd been warned about was indeed true. He was a predator and was only using me.

I realized that everything I'd been warned about was indeed true. He was a predator and was only using me.

At exactly that moment, my mom walked into the study, unaware of what was happening.

"I think you two need to talk," my dad said.

My mom and I went upstairs to my bedroom, and I opened up to her about my relationship with Aadam for the first time. I have to say it felt good to have a real, honest conversation with my mom. It was the first time it had happened in months. It also felt a little weird to be telling her about Aadam, after I'd kept him a secret for so long. It felt good to come clean about my relationship with him. My anxiety melted away and I felt something I hadn't felt in a long time—peace. As my mom and I kept talking and bonding, the gap I'd felt between us for so long was closing fast. I knew then that she'd never turn away from me.

For the past several months I'd felt like I was in over my head and couldn't get out, I explained to her, and Aadam had been very controlling to keep me in the relationship. He was the one who discouraged me from going skydiving, scuba diving, and riding a motorcycle. He advised me on what to eat, what to wear, and how to act. He was the one who encouraged me to abandon my friends because they were Christian and acted differently than he thought they should. I admitted that Aadam often became mad at me, and I could sense when his anger was rising.

My mom explained what a real boyfriend should be, and she reminded me that someone who cared for me wouldn't try to control me but would be alongside me in experiencing new things and be a good partner. And she told me that when one person is dominant, that never makes for a healthy relationship. Finally, she explained that the FBI agents didn't have ulterior motives in warning me about Aadam. They had lived it, seen it, and worked these kinds of cases every day. She and my dad only wanted me to be happy and safe.

"Aadam is the only one who has an ulterior motive, and he will tell you whatever he needs to tell you to get you back," she said.

During my conversation with my mom, I was texting with Aadam off and on. Based on my facial expressions, my mom suspected that something was going on. She explained that four things would probably happen if Aadam sensed that I was trying to pull away from him. He would either play the sympathy card, in which he'd ask, "How could you do this to me?" He'd play the guilt card and ask, "After all I've done, you're doing this?" He'd play the love card and say, "I love you! You can't leave me!" Or he'd play the anger card and say, "I've spent a year with you, how dare you do this!" My mom predicted Aadam would use every trick in the book to try to regain control of me.

> At that moment, I realized there was probably nothing unique or special about our relationship. He'd probably used the same tactics on other girls.

Once my mom said that, I glanced at her with a confused look. As I looked back at my text messages with Aadam, I began to realize that he'd already used each of those tactics with me. It was further confirmation of what Agent Sheridan said about his behavior being predictable, and it was yet another confirmation that Aadam was not who he said he was. At that moment, I realized there was probably nothing unique or special about our relationship. In fact, he'd probably used the same tactics on other girls.

My mom, I think, was sensing that I was afraid and unsure of what to do, and she asked me if I felt lost. I told her that I'd always had a goal or something to look forward to, whether it was working with whales, getting a macaw, or going to Kosovo to be with Aadam.

Now I didn't feel a sense of direction in my life. In a lot of ways, I felt like I was adrift.

My mom told me she'd scheduled a counseling session for our family later that week, but that I was welcome to use it as an individual session. I softly admitted I could probably use some help in getting my life back on track.

After my conversation with my mom, I was able to gain real confidence in myself. I knew I had to tell Aadam that we couldn't be together, but I dreaded doing it. For whatever reason, I still felt like I should be loyal to him, and I hated making him mad. But I was finally starting to realize that my family were the ones who loved me. I typed out a text message to him:

> Aadam: I'm sorry but we can't do this any longer. I've tried to do everything I could, but it just isn't working and I'm tired. This is so painful to do, but I can't hurt my family any longer. I'm sorry but I will not speak to you again.

Through tears, I finished typing the message I never imagined I'd write. My finger hovered over the "send" button on my cell phone for a few minutes. Like when I hesitated about buying a plane ticket to travel to Kosovo to marry him, hitting "send" meant so much more. This time, it was about saying good-bye to someone I was certain I had loved. For so long, I had felt like I needed to be with him, but now I was ending our relationship. Hitting "send" meant I would never meet Aadam, but it also meant freedom. I could finally be the person I had been suppressing for a long time, and I could have back the family I missed so dearly.

I dried my tears on my sleeve, took a shaky deep breath, and pressed "send" on my phone. I sobbed as I blocked Aadam on my phone, Facebook, and everything else I could think of. I knew it was better this way and was something I had to do. It was over.

The next morning, I ran downstairs like I hadn't done in months. I sat down on the couch with my parents, and looked at them with a newfound light-heartedness. I felt as if a hundred pounds had been lifted off me. I felt like I could even breathe easier, and for the first time in a long time, I knew things were truly going to be okay.

> I sobbed as I blocked Aadam on my phone and Facebook. I knew it was better this way and was something I had to do. It was over.

"Well, I did it," I told them. "I broke up with him."

I was almost gone, but now our nightmare was finally over. It was time for me to move on with the rest of my life.

CHAPTER 25

Acceptance

John

Surprisingly, Mackenzie waited six months after our final meeting with Agent Sheridan to finally ask us how we knew about her plan, who told us about it, and what transpired behind the scenes as Stephanie and I frantically worked to stop her from leaving. Make no mistake: rebuilding our relationship with Mack and learning to trust her again wasn't easy. But with God's guidance, we were able to do so with time.

One morning, about eight months after Mackenzie ended her relationship with Aadam, I took her out to breakfast at a local restaurant. As we ate breakfast tacos, I looked at her and said I needed to tell her something important. As far as her mother and I were concerned, I explained, everything that happened was in the past and we were moving forward. All was forgiven, and now it was time for her to forgive herself.

Sitting in a crowded restaurant on a steel stool, Mack quietly expressed her remorse for doing what she'd done. She also expressed fear that others would one day find out. I took her hand and tried to comfort her with some words of advice.

"You can either spend the rest of your life trying to hide this from people and always being afraid they'll find out, or you can own it," I said. "It's now part of your past, and it's never going away. The best thing you can do is to try to make something good out of it. If you can help one girl or one family by sharing your experience, then you would be paying it forward, and that's the best thing you can do."

> **"You can either spend the rest of your life trying to hide this from people and always being afraid they'll find out, or you can own it."**

I'm happy to say that Mackenzie has owned her mistakes, learned from them, and is now leading a happy, productive life. I couldn't be more proud of what she's done to earn back our trust and the direction her life is now headed. Of course, at the time of that breakfast, I had no idea we'd one day be writing this book together. But, after having gone through this wonderful writing experience, she has come to appreciate the power and beauty of paying forward the many blessings she has received, and so have I.

From May 13, 2014, to June 7, 2014, Stephanie and I had twenty-five days to save our daughter. That was the time we had from when we first learned about Mackenzie's plan to secretly leave the country until the day she planned to board a plane to Kosovo to marry a man she'd never met.

Only twenty-five days separated us from losing our daughter—possibly forever. We had twenty-five days to figure out the details of her secret plan, devise a counterplan, and then carefully execute it.

Remarkably, twenty-five days was just enough time for us to get it done, and those twenty-five days proved to be priceless in keeping Mackenzie safe.

Stephanie and I know we wouldn't have had twenty-five days if three of Mackenzie's high school friends hadn't come forward and said, "Somebody needs to know." Six months after Mack broke off her relationship with Aadam, we met with Jordyn and Madison to individually thank them for having the courage to step forward and warn us about what she was planning. We presented each of them with a gift that we hoped would symbolize our deep gratitude. We gave each of the girls a necklace with a round silver pendant with their first initial inscribed on the front; "2 Co 9:15" was inscribed on the back.

Sarah was attending college out of state, so we mailed her the gift, along with a letter that captured our face-to-face meetings with the other girls. It read:

Dear Sarah,

As 2014 came to a happy ending for our family, Stephanie and I reflected on how close this year came to being tragically different. Mackenzie is alive today because she had a friend who loved her and possessed the courage and wisdom to come forward to let her dad know what she was planning to do. You should know we have not revealed to Mackenzie how we came to know of her plan. While we believe that she would now accept this with gratitude, we will leave this decision to you alone.

Your decision to come forward gave us precious time to formulate a plan, to get help, and by God's grace, to bring her back into the arms of her loving family. Today, Mackenzie is closer to her family than she has been in many years. She is happy and she is safe.

Sarah, we can never fully express the depth of our gratitude to you, but we hope this small gift will help. If you haven't already, please open it now before reading on.

The verse inscribed on the back, 2 Corinthians 9:15, says: "Thanks be to God for his indescribable gift." This verse has dual meaning to us. First, God put you in Mackenzie's life for a reason, and you honored that by saving her life. Your gift to Mackenzie transcends the words we are able to speak or write. Stephanie and I can only whisper, "Thank you."

The second meaning for this verse goes back 19 years to when Mackenzie was only a few months old. We commemorated our first child's arrival with an heirloom clock that stands in our home today. It has a bright brass pendulum, which is engraved with Mackenzie's initials. At the base of this clock is a small brass plate that is inscribed with her "life verse" that we carefully selected and was read at her baby dedication ceremony—2 Corinthians 9:15.

And so it goes. God's wisdom and grace comes full circle. Words are not enough. Thank you for your "indescribable gift" to Mackenzie and to our family.

Love,
John and Stephanie

It was many more weeks before Madison, Jordyn, and Sarah, each in their own time, told Mackenzie that they had come forward to help save her. While Mackenzie is once again socially active and now likes to be around a lot of people, she will never forget that she has three friends who stand above all others, three friends who love her, and only three friends who put her well-being above themselves. We gave away three necklaces to thank three remarkable young women.

Each of those girls expressed similar sentiments to us: "I would not have been able to live with myself if something had happened to her." Love is kind and giving and selfless, and each of those three young women personifies those attributes. Mackenzie has three friends in her life who truly love her. Our hope is she never forgets it and always keeps them in her life.

I close this story thanking our Lord and Savior Jesus Christ, who was beside us throughout this remarkable journey. How did Christ help us? For Mackenzie, it was through a trio of friends who loved her more than they loved their friendship with her. For us, it was through friends who didn't blink when we needed help, a network of prayerful support, and a family that supported us through thick and thin. It was also through a pair of FBI agents who cared deeply that our daughter was safe, through a faith-based marriage that withstood the violent storm, and through a loving wife who is also my closest friend.

Along the way, I received words of wisdom from numerous people, none of whom would have touched me without God's hand. There was the BBQ joint owner who told me to "love her where she's at." There was a counselor who reminded me, "It's not about you," and a loving brother who told me to "rely on your faith." There was a pastor who silently sat next to a sobbing father and told me, "What will bring her back is a Father's love," and a Savior who taught me to tell my remorseful daughter, "All is forgiven."

Mackenzie

The day the FBI agents confronted me at the dining room table in my parents' home was definitely a turning point in my life. It wasn't until several months later that I learned how much my parents knew about my plans to travel to Kosovo and marry Aadam and the extraordinary lengths they went to to save me and stop me from going.

Coming out of such a dysfunctional relationship wasn't easy, but the "intervention" of the FBI agents and the dogged support of my parents were the forces I needed to get me moving in the right direction. I went through a long period of recovery, which included a lot of time with a counselor.

It took me a while to get over the initial shock of what happened. I could hardly believe Aadam had lied to me the entire time. He was not only a stranger, but also someone who had no intention of loving me. When I was first told about what the FBI and the mosque had discovered, I kept thinking about the small chance that maybe, just maybe, they were wrong about him. How could someone I'd spent every day talking to be a completely different person than he'd said? I was shattered, and I felt the most alone I have ever felt. I'd sit in my room at night and cry for hours. I felt betrayed and like a fool.

For a while, it felt like my entire world was crashing down around me. I had lost my friends, ruined my senior year of high school, and badly damaged my relationship with my parents. The silver lining in everything that happened was that my parents didn't give up on me. In fact, it was quite the opposite. When I was struggling the most, they checked on me and continued to care for me, which really struck me. After I put them through a year of hell, I thought for sure they would be done with me, especially after they learned I was preparing to leave them. But they continued to love me no matter what, and that was the first time I started to see the light. I started thinking that maybe my parents had my well-being at heart the entire time.

Before I could forgive myself, I had to realize that it's okay to be embarrassed. I was so ashamed of what I did for a long time; even the mere thought of telling someone my story made my stomach turn. I didn't want to think about it, talk about it, or have any reminder of what I did—and almost did. I kept thinking people would judge me for leaving the Christian faith and getting so lost.

> Before I could forgive myself, I had to realize that it's okay to be embarrassed.

I'm sure there are people out there who will judge me even now, but if there's one thing I've learned the past few years while reflecting and writing about my experience, it's that it doesn't matter whether or not people judge me. With time, I've learned to accept my mistakes, and I've learned *from* my mistakes. I know I can't ignore and not think about what I did. Instead, I've accepted what happened and tried to make something better out of it.

Before I could move forward in my life, I had to determine the answers to the questions that had consumed me for a while. How did I reach a point where I was not only willing, but also *wanting*, to turn away from everything I had known? What would have inspired me to walk away from my parents' love, my younger brothers, my friends, and everything I had been taught and believed? Taking a step back and looking at this from a distance, it is hard to believe that I could be so serious about leaving my home forever to be with someone I had never met, especially someone who put so much guilt and pressure on me. I'm sure it sounds crazy to so many people.

Being such an independent and strong-willed person, it is also hard for me to believe—even now—that I ever reached such a dark place.

As I started my recovery, I thought more deeply about how I became involved with Aadam to begin with. Based on my research and counseling, I realized he created a codependence, which has been described by some medical experts as "relationship addiction" in situations like mine. That description certainly fits the connection I had with Aadam. I spent months talking with him and was reluctant to end our relationship, even after I noticed obvious warning signs. It was never clear to me that he was manipulating me. He had the ability to convince me that everything he said was the truth and what everyone else was telling me was wrong. When I look at the difficulty I had in breaking away from Aadam and the extremely tight grip he had on me, I see the level of dependence I had on him.

Even after everything that happened, I have to admit that the time I spent with Aadam was very exciting. He was unique, mysterious, and he seemed to care deeply about me—at least that's what I felt at the time. I was physically and emotionally attracted to him, and he had a way of keeping me interested. Even when he started treating me badly or was very controlling, I was already so emotionally invested in him that I couldn't walk away, even when I wanted to.

One of the big factors in my conversion to Islam was my involvement at the mosque. After I started worshipping at the mosque, so many people surrounded me, and that made it even harder to break loose. Now, when I drive past the mosque, I can't help but stare. I feel so many emotions when I see the place: anger, sadness, brokenness, but truly nothing good. As I've gotten older, I've been able to see things in a different light. I have come to realize that I was not fully truthful to the people at the mosque, and in a lot of ways I did use them to hear what I wanted to hear. I should have told them the truth about how Aadam and I met, but I chose to surround myself with people telling me that what I was doing was acceptable. However, I have also come to understand that the people at the mosque could have—and should have—handled things differently as well. Because I was a high school student looking to flee the country without my parents' knowledge, I feel my plans should have been discouraged from the very beginning, or at least handled differently.

Everything I thought was real wasn't what I thought it was, or just simply wasn't anything at all. I think that's what that year with Aadam really was—an illusion.

After I began to see the truth, I was angry that I'd wasted a year of my life on someone like Aadam; even so, I gained some good things from that year. I have a stronger relationship with my parents and my brothers than ever. I have an incredible story that I can use to educate young people about the dangers in the world, and I hope I'll help save lives in the process. From my family, I've come to understand the true meaning of love and forgiveness, and from my three special friends, I've seen what true friendship really means. Most importantly, I have more faith in my Savior, Jesus Christ, than ever before.

After coming to grips with what occurred, I eventually started putting my energy into new activities that challenged me. I started riding motorcycles, then got my skydiving license, and now I am starting my junior year of college. I am pursuing a double major in psychology and child development. The counseling that I received after that hard year played a significant role in helping me in my recovery, and I decided that I want to pay it forward for someone else. I also picked up my paintbrushes and canvas and started expressing myself through art again.

As Christmas 2014 was approaching, I thought about what I should give my parents. The previous holiday harbored so many bad memories for me and for them that I wanted to make new, good memories for us. After several weeks of thinking about what I should do, I decided to make them something I thought would show them how much I appreciated them, as well as what I had learned during the ordeal.

I bought a three-foot by two-foot canvas; maroon, khaki, and brown paint; and letter stencils. As I sat on the floor in my room one night, I started to paint what I hoped would perfectly sum up this wildly emotional story. I painted the canvas khaki and the corners a darker reddish brown. I glued gold leaves around the border and painted black butterflies dancing around text that boldly read: *"Family, where life begins and love never ends."*

After working on it for several hours, I sat back and smiled. I thought about everything my family and I had been through over the previous fourteen months. I knew they would forever be my protectors and they would never stop loving me.

Family means more and more to me each day, and I will never be able to repay my parents for what they did to save me. I have an incredibly strong family, amazing friends, and a patient, all-knowing God.

And *that* is truly an indescribable gift.

UNDERSTANDING AND HELPING LOVED ONES WHO ARE IN UNHEALTHY RELATIONSHIPS

My name is Cheryl La Mastra. I am a licensed professional counselor and have dealt with many teenage kids and the growing pains they and their parents go through during the adolescent years; and so among my counseling experiences are situations similar to the Baldwins'.

Whether you are a parent or a teen, you may be wondering how in the world anyone could get involved in an online romance with someone they've never met. But relationships beginning on social media sites are more prevalent than most realize. Dating sites make it easy for young, innocent teens looking for new relationships to connect. Predators and extremist groups are using social media to prey on adolescents and children at an alarming rate. Parents are often unaware of their child's involvement until it is too late—or as in Mackenzie's case, *almost* too late.

Thought Control

Thought control, or—as Mackenzie described it to me— "brainwashing" is an effective common technique that lures adolescents into exploring elusive relationships. Thought control is a systematic process that uses coercion to alter beliefs and attitudes by psychological means. It works by making preexisting beliefs and attitudes nonfunctional and then embedding new beliefs that serve the intentions of the perpetrator. The process begins with simple grooming to develop trust and keep the relationship secret. We see this clearly in Aadam's grooming of Mackenzie when he used guilt, manipulation, lying, and control to keep her dependent on him and disconnected from her previous relationships.

In developing a relationship, the perpetrator works diligently to alter the victim's beliefs, thoughts, and values by removing their freedom, independence, and decision-making abilities. Thought-control tactics include isolating the prey, encouraging a craving for constant connection, and breaking down loyalties with family and friends. As new beliefs develop through the addiction of the relationship, those new beliefs become the only acceptable and correct beliefs. The victim develops a unique trust in, passion for, and dependency on the perpetrator; and the victim takes on a new identity over the duration of the relationship. Again, we see this at work in Mackenzie's relationship with Aadam.

Why Adolescence Increases Susceptibility to Risky Behavior and Poor Decision Making

One of the first questions we need to answer is, *What makes an adolescent such an easy target?*

Physical and Brain-Based Changes during Adolescence

Adolescent teens experience both physical and brain-based changes that contribute to increased risk-taking behaviors and poor decision-making tendencies. These changes are *biological, cognitive, emotional,* and *motivational.*

The first contributor is *biological,* and it's known as puberty. During puberty, the body and brain undergo significant physical and emotional changes, which result in increased risk-taking and poor decision making—both of which have the potential to become addictive behaviors.

In addition to the physical changes that puberty brings, adolescents' brains are also changing: *cognitive, emotional,* and *motivational* changes heighten the teen's vulnerability to addictive behaviors involving alcohol, drugs, and even relationships.

Even though the *cognitive* portion of the brain is developing, adolescents still don't have the cognitive maturity to assess risks accurately.

Another factor in an adolescent's susceptibility to risky behavior and poor decision making is *emotional.* Adolescents typically push the limits, seeking pleasure and rewards that release dopamine, the feel-good hormone.

Both positive and negative emotions affect adolescents' decision-making and risk-taking mindset and can increase their defenselessness when it comes to addictive behaviors.

The emotional and physical high of obtaining immediate rewards becomes the *motivation* that drives an adolescent to think illogically and act on impulse.

We see an example of obsessive addiction in Mackenzie's relationship with Aadam. She says talking to him "was like a high. He was more important than friends and family." Relationship addiction has the same characteristics as a drug and alcohol addiction. Mack literally said, "He was like a drug," and when in contact with him, "sadness would melt away." She says, "I regained my confidence" and "I kept him hidden from everyone." There is no doubt that Mackenzie was addicted to Aadam and that her brain and body literally craved the "next fix."

Search for Identity and Individuation

Another thing that makes adolescents more susceptible to addictive behaviors is their very natural and healthy search for their personal identity and who they are as an individual: *Who am I? What do I believe? Why do I think and feel the way I do? Why am I here? What is the meaning of life?* These are all good questions. Adolescent development of identity is marked by exploration. This crucial part of development is called "individuation," and it is one of the most difficult times for adolescents, as they try to become more independent while staying connected and attached to the family. Balancing independence with family attachment isn't easy.

A negative or confused sense of identity, feelings of self-doubt, or lack of purpose or belonging makes adolescents vulnerable to those who would isolate and exploit them. Compounding these issues with feelings of guilt increases their susceptibility to predatory traps.

Both Mackenzie and her parents talk about Mack's innate personality traits of being strong-willed, adventurous, edgy, and even stubborn. While these are and can be great personality traits, they probably contributed to Mack's inability to assess the danger she was in. And because of these traits, her parents never dreamed she could succumb to manipulation and brainwashing.

Parents sometimes think that their child's personality protects them from exploitation. But this isn't always the case. The best advice I received as a young parent was from a police officer who worked the drug beat in our town. He told me some horrific stories, and I asked him to give me advice as to the signs I should look for in my own children. At the time, my sons were only three, four, and six years old, but I was thinking ahead.

He simply said, "Don't ever believe your kids won't do certain things. It's those parents who typically don't see the warning signs." In other words, don't put your head in the sand.

Parent-Adolescent Relationship

Few parents with grown children or teenagers will tell other parents that discord was absent during their child's adolescence. Conflict in the parent-adolescent relationship is a normal part of child-rearing, and can even help your child develop communication skills.

Parents who allow their adolescents to openly express personal thoughts and feelings provide opportunities to discuss complex viewpoints and talk about the difference between "safe" and "risky" behavior. When adolescents feel understood and heard, they are more likely to trust their parents, even when conflict arises. When they feel secure and connected in their relationship with their parents, they are more likely to transition to autonomy and adulthood in a healthy manner. But even with the best parenting, there are no guarantees.

The Baldwins had talked with Mackenzie about boys, appropriate use of phones and computers, and not accepting friendships on social media unless she knew the person. They had specifically talked to Mack about the dangers of Internet chat rooms; and yet, we saw how quickly Mack succumbed to manipulation and was "almost gone."

Identifying Contributing Factors

Relationships formed through social media sometimes become addictive, and there are certain key factors that make some people more prone to these relationships than others, so when parents, family, and friends are alert to these factors, they are better equipped to help.

Similar to substance-use addiction, individuals who are addicted to Internet, social media, and online relationships exhibit the compulsive desire to continually engage in the activity, regardless of its negative impacts on personal functionality (mental and/or physical) and on family, friends, and communal relationships.

Certain *personality traits* and *behaviors* as well as *psychological distress* can make individuals more vulnerable to online addictions.

Personality Traits

Research specific to both *Internet addiction* and *social-networking addiction* is continually improving in identifying personality traits that factor into behavioral addiction. Lewis Goldberg's research on personalities consolidated earlier discoveries of personalities to identify five primary factors. Those factors are *neuroticism, conscientiousness, extroversion, agreeableness,* and *openness to experience.* Here we'll look at the first three.

Individuals scoring high in neuroticism and low in conscientiousness are more susceptible to *Internet addiction,* while those scoring high in neuroticism and extroversion lean more toward *social-networking addiction.* Characteristics of neuroticism include moodiness, anxiety, worry, fear, anger, frustration, envy, jealousy, guilt, depressed mood, and loneliness. Emotional instability and problems concentrating are also more likely in individuals who score high in neuroticism.

Decreased conscientiousness often shows up as procrastination, lack of self-control, tendencies to antisocial behaviors, impulsivity, and unreliability. Low conscientiousness significantly aligns with the inability to achieve personal goals, which can lead to increased risk-taking.

Extroversion often shows up as being outgoing, needing to be the center of attention, being enthusiastic and action-oriented. Extroversion types engage frequently in social media and are more prone to addiction, which is commonly correlated with increased risk-taking and poor decision making.

Addictive Behaviors

A constant need to be connected to an online relationship inevitably brings about changes that parents, friends, and family members can be alert to. The most common behaviors are that the individual:

- becomes more secretive
- withdraws from family and friends
- has falling grades in most subjects, if not all
- changes personal appearance and beliefs
- noticeably changes attitudes and interest
- isolates self

People often describe the person who is swallowed in addiction as someone who just *changed*.

Other behaviors displayed by people entangled with addiction are:

- poor emotional regulation
- withdrawal

- excessive use of internet or social media
- difficulty engaging in goal-directed activities

Psychological Distress

Individuals who experience psychological distress are also at risk for online addiction. Psychological distress is unpleasant feelings or emotions that significantly decrease functionality in everyday life. An individual who has maladaptive coping strategies for normal everyday life stressors, who experiences trauma, or who endures a major life transition may succumb to psychological distress. Common symptoms include:

- trouble sleeping
- fatigue
- sadness
- memory problems
- avoidance of social activities
- weight gain
- irritability
- obsessive thoughts or compulsions
- reckless acts
- strange or abnormal behaviors
- hallucinations
- delusions
- belief that others hear their thoughts or that their thoughts are not their own
- distractibility and trouble concentrating

The effects of psychological distress potentially influence all areas of life, disrupting normal functionality that may propel a person to adopt addictive behaviors, such as Internet and/or social media addiction.

A Few Words to Teens

Please understand that in any addiction, *denial* is the number one problem! I give my clients an acronym for the word "denial": **D**on't **E**ven k**N**ow **I A**m **L**ying—*DENIAL*. Things that aren't good for us often feel right and part of the human condition. Or sometimes we excuse unhealthy behavior by telling ourselves *I am different* or *We are different*. This is *denial*.

There's a saying in the world of counseling: "I am as sick as my secrets." If, after reading the questions below, you see yourself or a friend going through these issues, please talk to an adult you trust about what is going on in your life. If you are reading this and have a friend who is in potential danger yet you are afraid of "snitching" to their parents or another adult, *stop* right now. Don't walk but run to get your friend help. Better to be a snitch than to have an injured or dead friend. The Baldwins are forever thankful to Mack's friends who came to them and saved Mack's life!

- Do you or a friend justify bad behavior, such as lying?
- Do you or a friend withdraw or get angry in order to make others feel responsible for your happiness?
- Are you or a friend afraid of making the person you're in a relationship with unhappy?
- Is the person you or a friend is in a relationship with trying to control you—such as wanting to know your every move, what you wear, where you are going, who you are going with, etc.?
- Do you or a friend find yourself withdrawing more and more from family, friends, and normal activities?

- Do you or a friend say to yourself, "Others don't understand me [or us] and how I feel"?
- Do you or a friend lie to cover up things in the relationship or even the relationship itself?
- Do you or a friend think that the person you're in a relationship with is the only one who understands you?
- Does the person threaten to leave you or a friend if he or she doesn't get their way?
- Is that person ever verbally, emotionally, and/or physically abusive?

Prevention and Intervention

Prevention is our first tool in combating the possibility of addictive behaviors and disingenuous relationships on the Internet.

Most parents talk to their kids about the appropriate use of the Internet. But technology now provides parents with the ability to track, monitor, and block software and apps on computers, phones, and tablets. A few tools available for parents to use to track, monitor, and block activity are:

- Net Nanny
- ChildwebGuardian
- CYBERsitter
- eBlaster
- Avira Social Network Protection

This list is not exhaustive, but it does provide a starting point for further research about specific products and services. Talking about the appropriate use of the Internet and social media is vital, but even more critical is talking about the predators lurking on the Internet and social media.

But what happens when preventative measures fail? *Intervention.* Parents, family members, friends, acquaintances, teachers, and anyone else who knows the person in danger can intercede at any point when drastic, abnormal, or unusual changes occur in behavior and/or personality.

The first option is to confront the individual about your concerns. Confrontation may be done individually, in pairs, or as a group. If the confronted person denies the behavior or noticed changes, then the next strategy might be a formal intervention, which involves a professionally trained interventionist or therapist. A formal intervention is strategically planned and allows extended family members to take part. Everyone who loves your addicted family member can come forward and say their piece to help your loved one move closer to treatment.

Knowing the right time to intervene is not typically crystal clear. The following points can be used as helpful guidelines in dealing with your teen, as well as help you personally:

- Seek a relationship with your teen above all. Author Josh McDowell has a great way of saying this: "Rules without relationship leads to rebellion."
- DON'T GIVE UP! No matter how many times your teen tells you to "leave me alone," trust your instincts.
- Don't be demeaning, shaming, or make personal attacks.
- Try not to use "absolute" words, such as "never" and "always."
- Remember what it was like to be a teen.
- Don't be afraid of putting consequences in place that hurt, such as turning off the Internet, taking their cell phone away, taking their car keys away, etc.

- Seek help, sooner rather than later. Things won't resolve on their own or fix themselves. Help comes in many forms: friends, relatives, pastors, or a therapist.
- A parent-teen relationship is built on trust, so respecting your teen's privacy is important. But when you see the warning signs as mentioned earlier in this chapter, it is time to snoop. As a parent, this is not only your right—it is your responsibility.
- As much as humanly possible, remain calm with your teen. The old saying "cooler heads prevail" is especially important with teens. Sometimes you just need to keep repeating your boundaries in a monotone voice so your teen will know you can't be manipulated by their anger or other tactics. Don't give in to anger.
- Remember, deep down inside, your teen really does long for you to hang in there. Keep trying and be there for him or her. Be lovingly relentless.
- Share with others for your own support. You may be surprised by what others have gone through. There is a lot to be said about common humanity. It lessens the shame and pain.
- Remember that no matter how hard you try, your teen will make his or her own choices that you have no control over.
- Let go. This may mean letting go of your dreams and hopes for your teen and leaving him or her in God's hands.
- *Keep your faith!* Being in continual crisis has a way of wearing parents out! Remember your values—God is on His throne, and He loves you and your child even more than you do.

The most important thing to remember when a family member or friend becomes captive to an addiction is to love the addicted person, providing encouragement and support. Acknowledging, accepting, and facing the problem is difficult, but working together in efforts of recovery, out of love and forgiveness, builds stronger relationships with a solid foundation. Hope remains, and the opportunity for positive change is possible with active involvement. If you have serious concerns, do not hesitate to address the individual, because that hard conversation may be the lifeline that saves a precious life.

Ephesians 4:15 is a verse from the Bible that has been a constant for me throughout my career, and it simply says: "Speak the truth in love." When we see a problem and choose to remain silent, nothing can change. But if we speak out in truth, with love as our motive, the possibility for change increases. Speaking harshly pushes people away, whereas speaking with love typically softens a person's heart—even if the confronted person doesn't like what is being said. "Speak the truth in love."

ACKNOWLEDGMENTS

John

When I began writing *Almost Gone*, my original intention was to ensure the story would never be diluted as time passes and memories fade. I wanted our children to know how Stephanie and I dealt with our biggest challenge so they would understand our foundation of faith in Christ, the value of friends and family, and know the importance of being able to forgive. It has been a fantastic experience to write this book with Mackenzie and Stephanie, even if it never got published. I wanted to write the story as well as I could, so through an online service, I met Melanie Davis, an independent editor and writer (Triumph Press), who coached us in writing the original manuscript. When I met Melanie for our initial meeting at a Starbucks in Garland, Texas, she listened intently as I recounted our story. Afterward, she suggested that I write the book with Mackenzie, promising me that if we did it together we'd find it to be a wonderful healing and learning experience for both of us. Melanie, you were absolutely right.

Stephanie, my wife and best friend, worked tirelessly with Mackenzie and me to help piece together the details of events big and small to paint as vivid a picture as we could—not only factually, but also emotionally. Of course, spending this much time on a project wouldn't have been possible without the support of everybody in the family, including our two sons Luke and Michael, who spent many breakfasts and dinners listening to "book talk." Additionally, siblings, Debbie, Jill, Paul, Phil, Kathy, and our parents surrounded us with their unwavering support, love, and prayers in the midst of our crisis. As you can imagine, I am proud and honored to have gone through this journey with my coauthor Mackenzie. When we wrote the original manuscript, we did so with the understanding that we would not publish if Mackenzie didn't want to do it. Mackenzie, it took remarkable courage for you to "own it," but you have. You came to realize and embrace that the best way to say thank you is to help someone else who is facing their own hardships, and that is the greatest gift you can give.

We had many friends who helped us bring our book to a national level, but it would not have happened without Ronelle Ianace. Ronelle heard Mackenzie and Stephanie share our testimony at a local Bible study and offered her support immediately. Ronelle, at the time, we couldn't have imagined how important and influential your help would be to us. Without Ronelle, we would have likely never met our outstanding agent, Nena Madonia Oshman, and the team at Dupree/Miller & Associates. Nena, thank you so much for pouring your passion, drive, and expertise into a couple of novice writers to bring our book out for all to read. Through Nena, we were introduced to Cindy Coloma, who developed our chapter layouts, provided expert suggestions, and built our formal proposal. Thank you both for everything you did to bring our book to new heights. Nena also partnered us with Simon & Schuster and our senior editor, Philis Boultinghouse, who have been an amazing team to work with.

Acknowledgments

Cheryl La Mastra, we greatly appreciate your professional expertise and the insights you shared in the "Understanding and Helping Loved Ones" section. We are confident that your expert analysis will help many other youths and parents facing a threat similar to ours.

We had a host of local support who provided us with encouragement, suggestions, and assistance. I'd be remiss not to thank Karsten Francis, our young marketing professional and webmaster; our good friend Jennifer Campbell, who was the very first to read our earliest manuscripts and provided great suggestions to make it so much stronger; and also Cora Estep for completing a separate manuscript review. We also want to thank my friend and highly talented photographer, Kori Pearson, who shot our family pictures used in the book, then insisted on donating her time and talents because she was so moved by the story.

Special Agent Kevin Sheridan, we will always be grateful for everything you did for our family. You were equal parts FBI expert and father; I'm honored to count you as a friend. Agent El-Sayed, thank you for your strong support whenever and wherever it was needed.

Finally, we thank our Lord and Savior Jesus Christ. Our prayer is that we responsibly and humbly use our story to minister to other families in their times of hardship to know how His unconditional love, grace, and hope can strengthen and sustain them, as it did us.

Mackenzie

I certainly echo my dad's comments above, but I would like to add a few appreciations of my own.

I'd like to acknowledge three people who are very important to me: Jordyn, Sarah, and Madison, you all played an important part in saving me in this story, but you've also played a crucial part in shaping who I am today. I would not be who I have become if it wasn't for your love, compassion, and forgiveness. You have taught me invaluable lessons, and I will never be able to express my gratitude for you. Thank you for loving me through the good and bad times. And thank you for welcoming me back with open arms.

I would also like to thank Special Agent Sheridan. You saw more than just a struggling, rebellious teenager. You saw and fought for me, as someone who needed help, even though I didn't want help. Many people have touched me through this journey the past few years, but Agent Sheridan, you have made a lasting impression on me. One day, I hope to impact someone as much as you have impacted me. Thank you for not giving up, and thank you for doing much more than you had to for someone you didn't even know. Without your help, I would not be here today.

Also to my family—oh, my family! What adventures we have been on. I am incredibly grateful to have the parents and brothers I do. You guys have given me endless support and love through everything we've been through and throughout this whole writing process. On the days I felt weak and scared to share this story, y'all built me up and showed me what good I can do with this. You have given me so much in so many ways. I cannot thank you all enough.

Lastly, I want to thank my father. We have spent so much time together in my lifetime, but writing this book has been a whole different experience for both of us. We have laughed, cried, and everything in between. You have shown me what a father's unconditional love is, and you have shown me how to be a confident, caring, and strong woman. We certainly share a unique bond, and I will treasure it forever. Thank you for taking the time to write, speak, and share this story with me. I most definitely could not have done any of this without you. I love you, Dad.